BNP

Best NEW Poets

2018

50 Poems from Emerging Writers

Guest Editor Kyle Dargan

Series Editor Jeb Livingood

This book was published in cooperation with *Meridian* (readmeridian.org) and the University of Virginia Press (upress.virginia.edu).

For additional information, visit us at
bestnewpoets.org
twitter.com/BestNewPoets
facebook.com/BestNewPoets

Cover and interior design elements originally by Atomicdust | atomicdust.com

Cover images: Sfio Cracho, stock.adobe.com
                    "Portrait of a Man," Art Institute of Chicago

Text set in Adobe Garamond Pro and Bodoni

Printed by Thomson-Shore, Dexter, Michigan

ISBN: 978-0997562323
ISSN: 1554-7019

Contents

About *Best New Poets*

Welcome to *Best New Poets 2018*, our fourteenth annual anthology of fifty poems from emerging writers. In *Best New Poets*, the term "emerging writer" is defined narrowly: we restrict our anthology to poets who have yet to publish a book-length collection of poetry. Our goal is to provide special encouragement and recognition to poets just starting in their careers, the many writing programs they attend, and the magazines that publish their work.

From February to May of 2018, *Best New Poets* accepted nominations from writing programs and magazines in the United States and Canada. Each magazine and program could nominate two writers, and those poets could send a free submission to the anthology. For a small entry fee, writers who had not received nominations could also submit poems as part of our open competition. Eligible poems were either published after January 1, 2017, or unpublished. Which means you are not only reading new poets in this book, but also some of their most recent work.

In all, we received over 2,000 submissions for a total of roughly 3,750 poems. A pool of readers and the series editor ranked these submissions, sending a few hundred selections to this year's guest editor, Kyle Dargan, who chose the final fifty poems that appear here.

Introduction

I think I will target this introduction toward those I am going to assume are mostly likely to read it: the contributors. This was an initially awkward project for me because I can just about remember (maybe even still feel) how deeply I rolled my eyes when the *Best New Poets* series was inaugurated. Not that I have never been a "new" or "emerging" poet myself (and we'll get back to that), but there is so much about "poe-biz" and the publishing industry that feeds on the beginning writers' desire for validation or for "breaking in"—the fetishizing of the "undiscovered." It is something I am particularly sensitive to as a mentor of people beginning their writing and publishing journeys. But I gave the series a chance, and have even nominated a number of poets over the years after I discovered it was housed in the same creative writing program where I got my start and that it was edited by a former professor of mine, Jeb Livingood. From what I have heard and seen, *Best New Poets* has been a welcome and encouraging addition to the literary scene, and I felt like I could not say "no" when the opportunity to guest edit a volume presented itself.

In this period of my life—as an artist and as a human being—I am beholden to the idea that life moves toward what we can imagine, or are actively imagining. And that idea is for me predicated on another: that what we see significantly influences what we can imagine. In her essay "Imagining the Unimagined Reader," one that remains perennially profound to me, Harryette Mullen writes the following:

> I write for myself and others. An other is anyone who is not me. Anyone who is not me is like me in some ways and unlike me in other ways. I write, optimistically, for an imagined audience of known and unknown readers. Many of my imagined readers have yet to encounter my work. Most of them are not even born yet. About one-third of my pleasure as a

writer comes from the work itself, the process of writing, a third from the response of my contemporaries, and another third in contemplating unknown readers who inhabit a future I will not live to see. When I read the words of African Americans who were slaves, I feel at once my similarity and difference. I experience simultaneously a continuity and a discontinuity with the past, which I imagine is similar to that of the unborn reader who might encounter my work in some possible future.

I am enamored with the idea of "possible futures" as opposed to alternate futures or realities—which I think about a lot (like the one in which I took my uncle's advice about training to play tennis professionally and am likely married to Serena Williams and retired by now) but have a sense of randomness. There is something intentional about the events that realize "possible futures," and to that effect I saw my work in editing this volume of *Best New Poets* as curating work for—or toward—a possible future. And what of the now did I want the future to see that we were wrestling with, reckoning with? That would be our inadequacy when it comes to a) accepting and negotiating plurality and b) confronting our history with, and sustained normalizing of, physical and sexual violence against each other, and against women in particular. And I sacrificed no craft standards (especially my own firm standards for lineation) in assembling this work. For a poem to have what it is attempting to say taken seriously, it must *say* attentively and seriously.

I hope all the poets, be it their first or third and final time published in the series, hold on to this moment—this appreciation of their early work as poets. It is fairly easy for us to find our way into writing one poem, but to do it again and again over time (and against your own anxieties and evolving expectations for your own writing) takes it toll. And I do not think most people hear that when they are beginning to write and publish—or (and here is the return mentioned earlier) no one told it to me. Had they, I would have appreciated more my "emerging" period and the poet I was then. I would have thought more about my pace and for whom exactly I was pushing myself to produce. And maybe now more than ever—in this "content"-hungry moment when creators and their human needs are more afterthought—such introspection is valuable and healthy.

Again, these poems buoy my faith that notedly and necessarily different possible futures will come—that the work is being done to deliver us there. And still, for the futures near enough to one day host us, what shape will we all be in when they arrive? I think about the Civil Rights Movement often, and how broken and warped many of its leaders became by the time elements of their possible futures arrived—how in those futures some who were once leaders turned into exploiters because that is how they chose to process their pain. For those questioning this allusion, no, poets are not inherently activists. But they are seers who many activists' imaginations have followed. We need both. We need all. Thank you for this work. And as this history advances, please be kind to yourselves and to your art. I find myself saying this almost every day to someone struggling with the psychic weight of this moment. It may be *possible* that we don't have to destroy ourselves today after today to make the tomorrow we need. "Nothing ventured," no?

—Kyle Dargan, 2018 Guest Editor

Chelsea Bunn
Litany

Survived the father's
the kitchen table
hand of passing
snaking
open hand of young
corner/Mexico
man dragging leathered
my lifeless form
hands/my neck
read my diary
across the aisle
in the unsound dark
a plague/a sore/a curse
the light that flickered
and banged us to a stop
in Brooklyn
the door that delivered me
the night
its resilience
its resolve
its tender grief
the garbage disposal
the neat waste it makes

hand across
that sudden sting
man/Canal Street
up my skirt
boy/crowded
twenty-three/older
hands across
high school boy's
I wouldn't let him
city bus/man
busying his hand
his gaze a stain
but praise
overhead
somewhere
and praise
into
and praise the body
and praise the body
and praise the body
and praise
of the mind
of scraps

Hannah Perrin King
Architecture of Descending

> *I didn't jump to save my life, she told me…"I jumped to save my body, because if I stayed inside the factory I would burn to ash, and my family wouldn't be able to identify my body."*

Angels don't have wings, angels fall up. Girls make their wings out of skirts on the way down. They pull their skirts into bells and ring the smoke. One hundred and one years of girls flying on their skirts, or pallus, or hair. Modest and arrowed, like osprey—like hunters. A hunter to hunt must pick the fat off the bones—the waxen bubbling—before she breaks them, must latch her hooks to smoke, and believe in the un-gravity of mathematics: that for each numerically negative trajectory, there exists its opposite. That they are the same. A mirror, on its back, reflecting sky. Point of axis, infinitely reflected. Three to five to eleven stories below, the concrete salts its skin, opens its jaws. Lipped, and yowling. Each hit, each thud, a point of axis. Of entry. Angels do not have wings. Angels are broken girl bodies identified by their mothers. Angels are ash of blazing factories collected onto the roofs by the buckets into the palms of fathers, brothers, sisters. The sons yowl, the mothers grind unpolished glass, the textiles burn. A good hunter was once the hunted. x, y: x over y, two small wings. Too small wings. Angels are mirrors where there is cement. The smoke chases its tail. The girls fall to their wings.

Jennie Malboeuf
The Men

are calling again.
The men look through my purse.
The men follow me home
block after block of treelined
streets from the library or the bar,
cussing *cunt cunt cunt*
a few steps behind.
The men hand me green apples,
saying *they're sweet, you're sweet.*
The men tell me they know me.
That they could sleep better
if I'd *just lay beside* them
in the tiny bed. They hurl the word
independent like an insult.
The men feed me evenings.
Worry. Warm beer to the side
of my mouth. One compliment.
The men ask me if I can *conjugate amo*?
They invite friends over
and put their arm around her,
my hand between their legs.
The men stop calling because my being
Catholic is *too much*. The gold trimmed
cards of Mary watch them from the wall.
The men boast how they like us fat,
skinny, thick, short, blond-haired, black.
The men get mad when I teach myself to come

to what makes me jealous, when I ask
them to tell me what happens in the movies
they watch, when I can't come to
anything but the fantasies they have.

Michael Lee
At the Lake

you will never touch again,
I offer myself myself,
reach to sever the same water
by which I am severed, hewn
by the wide blue blade.
Only my shadow touches
land, the shadow its own
departure, the way light
is the only witness to
what it touches, and cannot
itself be seen. Only what it illuminates:
a single sparrow studying
nightfall, learning nothing
about nothing until its body,
and song—its most dedicated
scholarship—are gone. Still
in their absence, there was a boy
and then there wasn't.
His shadow broke free
like a single witness refusing
to witness anymore, running
darkly away, the shadow
so light on its feet it seems
we would call it flight
if it would simply lift off the hot grass.
The shadow is everything
removed, the shadow is proof
of what light cannot do
and what terrible things
we have done beneath it.

Kathryn Hargett
Leda & the Swan

After Richard Siken // For J. & T.

Every morning the stones on the sternum: opening.
    Every morning another chapter where the hero
        is a woman slurred between forested fatigues, the flesh of her stomach
unspooling into yarn.
              Who is the cannibal now?
    Every morning the birds falling backwards into the sky
        like a film in reverse, the feathers collapsing
            in my palms to rosary beads.
    How I could bless the sin out of my ribs—
Dear So-and-So: I'm sorry I never answered your calls.
Dear So-and-So: I'm sorry I answered your call
    & wept like a storm drain for six years, the receiver
        a canefield emptied of its plumage.
                You want a better story.
                I understand.
           Who wants to hear a story
             where the subject
                is an empty room, a closed door?
The mountains in Fujian, then, where some grandmother of mine
    incubates herself with a prayer softened by waiting, her soldier sons
        folded beneath her sternum. Like a nun, running, on fire,
her white blouse spread across the stone pillars
        like mist into the lungs. Or Victory Strikes
    lifted to my grandfather's lips
        to bless himself out of the air,
            burn the night sky into prophecy:
           an augur
           scrying for his daughter's pallid face.

Or
a woman in a San Francisco night, her black eyes
    gleaming like Orion, rising to meet you.
        Her red dress unfurling beneath your hands.

Dear So-and-So: you've never been to San Francisco,
    & this is not a happy ending.
Dear So-and-So: there is no happy ending,
        no slain dragon or high priestess or gleaming knight
    waiting at the end of this sentence
      to gather you against their breast, kiss you on both
    of your cheeks, everyone weeping, everyone saying,
my dear So-and-So, we were just kidding,
        real life is so much better than this.

Dear So-and-So, when we were in the psych ward
    everyone asked us what we wanted to be when we grew up
      & everyone said *happy* but we all meant *autocannibal.*
I remember all those boys with eyes that say *Run, Run, Run.*
Dear So-and-So, I remember the story so well.
    Your lips brown & chapped like the bark of a baobab,
      our palms coated with patina. How we sat in the sun
and watched birds plummet, beak-first, into the concrete,
    Apollo blazing the sun through our hands.
      So-and-So, they called me *dogeater* & *Philomela,*
      tongue dissolving through my fingers
    into Atlantic spume, all my dead friends
passing through me like a summer wind. My neck
    a cardinal between their teeth.
That day someone had tried to smash the psychiatric windows
    like shucking a coconut,
        then cut himself open
          & fleshed into the ground.

So-and-So, these were the first stones.
    Dear So-and-So:
        here is the day where you call my mouth *aripiprazol*
    & tear your cousins into roots. Here is your tongue, not a tongue.
        Your body unsure if it wants to become a body.
    Here's the moment you named *serotonin*, a torch
        whittled between your lips. Here's the day I left you
    alone in a gray dome, condensation gathering on your temples,
        I'm sorry, I'm sorry—
Dear Forgiveness:
        sit down at the table
        & let me anoint you with patchouli & salts.
    Dear Forgiveness:
        Won't you come in, scorch the ward
                into a cathedral
        of red-lipped sky.
I know, So-and-So. The world is a big place.
        We were all just kidding.
        Come in.
             There are so many things I want to tell you.

Shakthi Shrima
There are always birds

trying to come inside. I came inside. The door was half-
open, the living room floor dressed in a flurry of feathers. A bird

had burst in, sure that a room must be like any other place—
but then my house with its beast's jaw. Its hunger. Its practiced

growl and whir. The bird swelled
with fear and shit everywhere, I mean

everywhere, carpets a splattered dictionary of panic.
I found it huddled with the dishtowels, shivering.

Later I asked, *why the dishtowels.* My mother said
they must have been the right kind of soft. Like a nest, or grass—

grass, the softest thing we all share. And the bird a heartbeat
threatening the sky. We cradled it to our chests in turns,

watched it flutter frantic and dissolve in the street's chant
of rooftops. Before this, another bird, brown, broken-necked,

limp at the lip of the garage. My father gathered it
into a dustpan. I did not watch. And the first bird, a sound

gathered ruthless into a fist and rushing at the window
as though it were air, beat at the pane, once—

To fly must be to defeat the body. To live everywhere
and nowhere. John, I've been having this dream:

your room has grown into a house, complete with cement
scars and a screen door. Outside, the punched

plums stinking, the finches snatching away
their secrets. The room is just as it was. Nothing there

but the slump of my body pinned beneath the dark
canopy of your grunting. One word and only my mouth

to forget it. My sternum a column of claws. John,
I was so small to you, which would explain

why I felt too heavy to move, too still to want or not want.
In the dream we're on the porch, some bird bleeding

out in the grass: sparrow, kestrel. Does it matter?
A rack of bullets limps your right hand. The jets spit

into the lazy sky. The bird isn't dead yet.
I invent a glint in its mouth's gun-dark

every time I have the dream. Its body's curdle
and twitch. Any sign. I never go closer

to the bird, never try. At least the afternoon's cool
thrum. At least the grass, soft. Our house whirs

and you wrench me into it. You say, *come in
now.* Even after I wake I am thinking of the bird.

How I would have forgotten it if it were whole,
unbroken. Miraculous, how its heart flocked

fluent into the dirt. It bled
and bled. It bled because it could.

*

Tonight I am red for a world paled
of red. I walk around like a tooth

in a mouth that's still laving over a bitten
tongue. My collarbones are proud

as knives. The dark is a dark which quarters
everyone like melons. I kiss up one strange soft

gift of skin, then another, quick,
my brain blackened with light, I kiss all the way

to the softest skin I can find, I try
to keep it. I cannot keep it. All the way and still

I cannot stop. I want and want. I'm shivering. A limp
pair of wings against hard glass. I can't help it. I couldn't

help it. I had to burst through the door,
empty myself anywhere I could. My body

had to come in from the crooked
sky. Had to stumble crooked through the house

to see if the house would whisper back, or twitch
to life. Any sign. Isn't that how it goes, John?

Enter something and you become it. In the dream
you shot the bird because because you could. Tonight,

I look down at your clenching hands, hung
suddenly from my crooked wrists. In my heart

is a screen door with me on one side,
every open beak I have ever known on the other.

They rush at me cawing, tongues thrumming
with blood, claiming freedom, calling *join us, join us.*

Kristen Renee Miller
A Billon Things in One

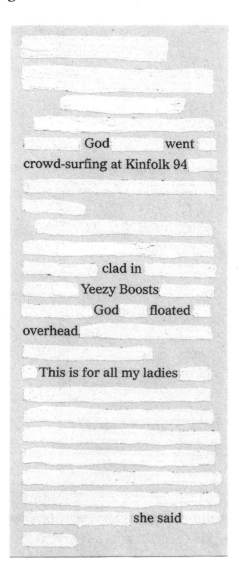

God   went
crowd-surfing at Kinfolk 94

clad in
Yeezy Boosts
God   floated
overhead.

This is for all my ladies

she said

While few

    may know   God

    her   followers

are

    often

celebrities

She   gets name-checked

in rap songs

Which is fine.

This is what you see if you
follow
God

God
the always-on

the   #NeverNotWorking

lit from below

with

an external
battery pack

called   Queen of

                Highsnobiety

voice of Generation Y
                'It' girl
the Millennial dream

Instagram

selfie   God

never-

ending party

God

God

with Disney

princess eyes

'What am I?   God

said

in

    h   e r

turtle

                        down   coat

        I'm a

billion things in one

We are literally

you r

curren   c

y

sa

ng

a couple hundred

thousand people

God   raised her iPhone

                        and   in

                turn

                                the crowd

                filmed her filming them

        too

"A Billion Things in One" is an erasure poem created from a single newspaper article, "Meet YesJulz, Snapchat Royalty," by Max Berlinger, which appeared in *The New York Times* on June 28, 2016.

Noor Ibn Najam
train

before tears break surface
tension with their weight

head-on, we argue
about my gender, again

all of me is illuminated
no shadows. i don't think

we're the same. he's level
tones, voice of metal

like a man, i break
my voicebox open. he hears

the doppler effect.
we can't stop now

even when bones and
skin break. i'm made of

bright emotion
against welded reason

my old name
the one he keeps,

i feel baba's pupils
bright as headlights

he's scoffing
and for a moment

in the yellow light
in his high beam eyes

i argue, in ricocheting
pitch, he never quivers

i'm a child, i'm young again
a low whistle approaching

the collision will be head-on.
we won't make a sound—

hot nerve—his logic—cold
steel, i'm colorfully bruised

i lose the argument
i can't defend. i fold back into

girl
framed in silver. now i'm

out of sight

Teresa Dzieglewicz

We End Up at a Buffalo Butchering after the Halloween Party

Oceti Sakowin Camp, Standing Rock

Two men struggle, pull at the hide where its belly is slit like a seam, constellate
the thick fur with their headlamps, small beside the crude oil spotlights that bleach
the sky of stars now. A woman with a purple bandana slices the membrane,
exposed, thin as moon. The animal pops apart, knob-kneed, leg flung
toward the kids shivering in my lap. RJ whispers, "pilamaya'ye tatanka
for the stew and the taco meat." We nod, polyester ninja suits and tiger tails
dampening in the grass, snicker wrappers circling us like rocks around a fire.
Three days since Treaty Camp was raided, since I drove them in circles
all night past dark tipis and empty trailers, past ambulances clustered
like a scab by the waving flag road. All of us eating trunk-stale Oreos
and dry ramen, crooning too loud to some song nobody liked.
Everyone knew better than to ask for their family. I'm a zombie still.
Or half of one anyway, in dollar store make-up done up by the girls.
Shawnee Rae holds my face in her hands, delicate as if I'm a bundle
of bird bones, dabs baby wipes at the green sludge beneath my eyes, the blood
on my mouth. The buffalo's fat-frosted muscle glistens now, runs in streams,
the animal red and hideless in the too-bright night. "We look like that inside,"
Shawnee pauses to say. RJ says, "In the old days, they killed them with bows,
but now they use guns." Shaylena shakes her head, "No, only cops have those."

Phoebe Reeves
The Gardener and the Garden 23

Everything moves into
and out of the world

like breath. Like how
this little square of land

would look in aerial
time lapse—a breathing

in and out of colors.
Now heavy rains

have pushed the peonies
down, humbling

their faces to the ground,
and the once-

blooming rose is shedding
pink petals all

over the grass. I am so tired
and my sleep is

a leaky boat less sea-
worthy every year.

What will carry me
into the next

breath if not this bit of land,
where what can

no longer come to me
in dreams can still

emerge from earth
and flower?

Olatunde Osinaike
Mercy, Mercy Me

Eponym of burnt offering. Sinner simple. And to no one's surprise, I'm not a betting man. Though I would take myself in a heartbeat. Edgy as a canned good in the pantry, I pry open with obedience, this body I have. Yet like any good Wednesday, double

negatives take their time with me. And I elude. A domain of dominos and mustard seeds undone on my tongue. As if out of a parable, I was once found in the south, studying the aviation of snowflakes, how even in the darkness they can melt mid-flight. I was once told *try me.*

Then to speak it into existence. But I am clumsy. Whatever it was I do not recall. The funny things flaws become: shambles, soliloquy, spiritual. It was the same way I learned how to use *might could* in a sentence. And to this day I haven't let go of how I could taunt

a scythe with nothing more than some dirt and my brave lips. Oh, I can be such a mess when this world lets me. Gorgeous with sympathy. Nimble as an imperative. I submit because I care, too. Because I cannot trade away this audacity. Because so much can happen in a week. A horse loses a race. A race loses its culture. A culture loses its place. A place loses its race. Mothers lose their babies. Babies lose their wonder. If you ask me how I shall stay fed until the next first of the month, I would tell you I already

have a full-time job. If you ask what will keep me sane, I would want you to know I take vacation seriously like every good love story. Try me. In a game of charades where *making a snow angel* is as heavenly as it sounds. I can't even romanticize this part.

The thankless credential of raising a body from the dead. That it might could be yours, sometimes. How I've filled this life with disbelief in between. Lord, I'm not actually sure it's fair for me to assume you know where all the time goes.

Erika Mueller
Flight

This spring two thousand snow geese
drop from the sky into Mud Lake,
Idaho, and a young girl believes the sky
really has fallen, the beautiful cloud

of bodies drifting slowly in deep gray
water. They were trying to return
for summer, to the spot where they
first opened eyes. They can

find their way back. They also commit
to one life partner. So imagine when
one falls first, breathless on the steely
surface, cirrus scuffing its ebony eye.

And the other feels illness inside
herself, too, but must first mourn
her love, this departure, having to
face the last stretch alone.

In Alabama several teens tell a girl to commit
suicide or her family will all be killed.
Surely the teens are ill. Surely the young
girl, thirteen, imagines flight, lifting

herself away and heading home again.
Imagines too, what it would be

to stand in the cold, watching everyone
she's loved drop, one by one, around her.

And what of the man whose job it is
to lift each blossom of goose
from the water, its long neck draped
over his wrist or dangling like a noose,

drenched and sorry, its beautiful head?
For all of the hours he must look
for the white ruffs between ripples
and grasses, his eyes trained

on finding each fleck, hoping
the rest have made it. There are
those who don't want to believe
in such vulnerability, who laugh

wildly at the thought of this as a sign.
Some of us watch still images flash
on screens. A few see the call of spring
plummet into the eye of the lake, stand

crestfallen near last year's milkweeds.
The girl's mother contacts the school
and media. The State Department
of Fish and Game reports Avian Cholera,

contagion, quickly gathers the dead
and weak. Nearly twenty eagles watch
as the delicate meal they might have had
is scooped away like late snow,

the taste on their tongues, watch as the man
leaves and more convulse, surrender
in mirrored water, where some swim
erratic circles, mucous soiling their faces,
heads thrown far back between wings.

Amy Woolard
Mise En Place

The peonies are popping! A fist that is also a kettle that is also
A pact petals made with whatever cabal of bees decides to stick

Around. Let's all us shake on it. Ah, these lungs of mine the perfect
Emergency orange of extension cord coil. All my breathing is

Indoor/outdoor. Just be yourself, so I open a tab & order a
Whiskey, non-artisanal rocks. My sweat equity pays for itself.

Shoot, it only took half a second for it to get unpaid-electric-bill
Quiet up in here. The longing's prix fixe. Naturally, the peonies bang

Their way into the room, demand a table by the window. The city's
Swans give away the weather. Step out of the pond & into

The mix, swans! Make tracks like hatched forkprints on
Uncooked dough. Half a life is achieving a gorgeous crisp

Tear of a sugar packet's corner. Half a life is reaching
Casually for a dog who—sad to say—'s been gone for months.

—Nominated by *Virginia Quaterly Review*

Destiny O. Birdsong
Ode to My Body

after Lucille Clifton

you were born in the year of the rooster
& the dismembered   grandmother.

your mama's first christmas alone   trying to guess
how much sugar to put in the pies

& how much can kill.   you were bundled
into the house with the two uncles

sharing one of the bedrooms   & zero baths
(a summer cabin   in another life).

i have treated you like anything never earned:
every light blazing   fridge wide open

cooling the whole neighborhood.   doors unlocked.
i don't know   how you   survived

the years without sunscreen
or health insurance.   crabs from the first time

i dropped   (nameless
as apple seeds)   into the toilet.

the everclear.   the laxatives.   the Black-n-Milds.
you should have happened to a   more

careful woman.   never known
anxiety   or   shame

the thirteen-hour drive through arkansas   panic
silent as the sleet stickying the windshield.

the lectures taught with a gallon of Prep scouring
your insides   the distance to the bathroom tucked

behind one ear   my pride intent
on beating your best time.

if you could speak in languages
other than mucus & loose stools

i would apologize   for this   & other things
just to hear you answer   in a voice not unlike

my own   remind us what we are to each other:
echo   narcissus: both drunk on their own

guile.   both murderous in their
insistence   of love.

you should know   i never looked at you
& blamed your mother   though it is true

i have wished you smaller   with more symmetry
like the stone of a fruit nestled in the slick flesh

of the world.   in so many ways
i have tried   to discard you.

or i have   cut you in two
with water fasts   nicotine

stretched you to feed
the men   what they wanted

the women   what they could love.
& when you failed   (& i have called

you failure)   who could i blame?
what wonder is it   that your newest threat

is your own patrol of cells   —house divided
as the country   intent   on stealing

your coverage.   it's alright
that this is the most   epic thing about you.

& alright that   like your ancestors   you might leave
with fewer parts than   those with which you came.

i would promise you   good years
between now   & then   but who   would i

be fooling?   even now   i'm slipping you milk
&   slabs of bread   smeared

with butter.   like all your lovers
i know   how much you can take.

i have come to love   not you
but your   refusal   to be consumed.

i push you up   pill bottles & down stairs.
& every morning   you wrap a thin new layer

of membrane   around the sac that holds
my heart.   dispatch   a brigade

of cells with their   sealed   warrants
to a host of organs   i hope   i never see

Christine G. Adams
Ars Biologica: On Evening

The same walk home every evening
        as the neon signs of bars angrily hum
                and spit like grease in a pan. I am gathering

this new warm air in thimblefuls, to drink
        like a girl drinks from an empty teacup.
                I have swallowed all the nights

of my childhood the flood of dark
        along the plains, the air thick with reverb
                from cicadas in the grass, a twist of hissing,

glowing letters in a parking lot where
        my parents debated the ways
                of dipping french fries into milkshakes.

My mother says *like this*. My father echoes,
        his hands tracing a different path.
                All this evening. I'd like to believe

that what goes around comes back.
        The stippling of comets through space,
                an unreadable scoreboard for wins and losses.

I wrap the lopsided fluttering of a bird
        with a broken wing in a white sheet.
                I take her to a vet, who lays her flat

like a kite. Says *carpus, radius, tresses, pinion.*
        I hide these words under my tongue, each
                a remittance I might exchange for my dog's

long life. How the first cell split, and those two split again.
        How there was an Adam and an Eve.
                Life evens. An eye for an eye. Surprising,

always, how my shadow walks with me
        along the OPEN signs, the thudding bass
                timing our steps, how she disappears when

I turn the corner. In the morning, the sun
        will flesh out all the shadows, which is
                easy to forget. I am trying to remember

there is another day, warm and out of sight.
        There are two girls smoking on the sidewalk,
                posing in the cooling light. Tomorrow as distant

as Andromeda, enormous and spinning
        imperceptibly closer. They stumble.
                They *can't even.* I want to say that their spines

are strings, that they can pull them taut, find balance.
        It is all a circling back. We are going to end
                up the way we started. Yes, even me. Even you.

Chelsea Liston

Poem with Mars, God of War & Destruction &
Masculinity, as Beloved

(Field Guide)

The undressing isn't ceremonial. Watch—the tree
like a shivering woman shedding tufts of hair.

The bees don't mind, filling her up. Making
her noisy.

More flowers fall to the side of my face, bees still
writhing inside them.

I want to feel their abdomens rubbing
against each other, beneath my skin.

You lie next to me, your body draped
in god-glow. You tell me the flower's

scientific name, how easily it will kill me.

I don't know the Latin word for poison,

but when you say *poisonous*, I want it
on my tongue.

(*Common Offering*)

I lay the ram's ear over my tongue like a second skin.

It's March. All the lambs carved up on other tables,
I took a ram instead.

He was easy to lead. His horns inside my hands—

I felt the passage to his skull.

His lips darkened as he ate
blackberries out of my palm. I told him *I have always wanted*

a beautiful mouth. His mouth still

dark as I bent his neck
down towards the altar and cut.

Whatever forgiveness I meant to ask, I must ask

mute—my mouth full and still not pretty. Here,
help me

lace rosemary between his ribs before the fire cooks him.

(Mars, Lover)

The war between my ribs is also everywhere.

Stacks of feathers found in the snow, but the bird still missing.

You were born from the same animal
who first learned to stitch

a body into silence. It was comforting, your fingers
buttoning the fabric against my neck.

My throat, thinner. You show me, measuring its width,
forefinger and thumb.

You smear honey onto your lips and the wind carries

my yellow hair into their glue.

I imagine your nearness whenever I am most afraid
of you.   The way I feel

nests of spiders crawling down the hallway of
my throat, only after darkness hides them.

(Prophecy)

You stuck a candle down my mother's throat
and saw me

nestled in the pink cave of her, not yet ready to open
my fists.

My bald head shining like a terrifying orb. You stroked
the wet hair between my temples and felt

the dormant earth inside me:

its oceans foaming at their mouths. Its night sky clouded
with house fires, glimmering at a distance.

The future unfurling beneath your eyelids, you saw
my pelvic bone splitting at its center,

an expanse. How strange
you will look to me, if I ever learn

to spit all that earth out.

(Of War)

Spit it out for me. Let me hold it
in my cheek for at least one crawl around the sun.

I stand in the mirror clutching your spear, your laurels
sliding off my temples.

If I look for you without looking
for a fight,

where will I find you? I can't remember how

your skin tasted, sunned, saltly in
the July-hot morning.

Unarmed, your body becomes

a field I graze in. Lower

your head against mine.

Whatever is too heavy for my arms, let me carry
with my teeth.

(The October Horse)

I try not to look at its teeth, when the head
comes off.   It's October—

we sacrifice our favorite horse so you will
bless us. One by one,

we place its hollowed-out head over our faces and dance

for you. When my turn comes, I move the horse's tongue
like a puppet, and shift

my weight on my hips as if I am a just-born foal.

How lucky I am to know you, though you don't always
award me with the head. When it's over,

we cut the tail and soak it in the blood still pouring
from its neck.   Tail-as-brush, we paint

anything we hope to keep
secret—the blood drying quick behind my ears.

(Power Differential)

Let me speak one secret: I am tired
of folding my arms and legs

into the parcel of my girlhood.

You roll your tongue once, and this earth is
surrendered to you.

I spend the hours sculpting my mouth into
the beak of a rooster.

When you come home for me, I am almost

asleep. A dish rag
tied around my neck for decoration.

A single word embroidered on my shirt. *For-
lorn.* Touch me

nowhere—only I can

undress this body without ceremony.

Paulette Guerin
An Education

On TV when woman meets man
to try him out she asks him
to come up for a drink. That's code
for you can have sex with me,
not I really want to show you my African violet—
did you know that you can't touch the leaves
without hurting it? The man is polite and takes the drink,
acts amused by the décor, feigns interest
in the fragile African violet.
So if I ask someone up,
even if it is just to meet my cat,
he will think I'm sending a signal:
my body is yours. I will think, maybe
I'm supposed to send this signal, am supposed
to like another's footfall on the stairs,
his hand on the small of my back
as if to guide me, as if I don't know where I'm going,
as if I have to know where I'm going.

Anders Carlson-Wee
The Mark

Some say fire, some say language.
Some say God made us in his image
on the sixth day. Some say tools,

some religion. Some say whenever
we first dug a hole, marked
a grave—maybe the Neanderthal

family found in northern Spain:
skulls, ribs, jaws, a bowlful of teeth,
a nearly complete spine, a hand,

every carpal intact, arranged
below flowstone almost as in life.
Some say art, some crude representation.

Some say cooked caribou
catalyzed the boom in our brains.
Mother, father, child, infant.

Harris lines in the femurs told
how meager their meals were.
Their collarbones gnawed on, sawed

through, hacked at with flint tools,
ribcages crushed with something blunt
to get at the liver and marrow:

if they were buried they were buried
by their murderers. Some say up-
right gaits, opposable thumbs,

three-pound brains. Their skulls
cloven with engraved lithic blades.
The written word. Ritual.

Organs still warm in the middle.
Empathy. A sense of shame. Some say
we're still on the way to human.

T. J. McLemore
Desert Triptych

—*Christ in the Desert Monastery, Abiquiu, New Mexico*

The path down the Way of the Cross
isn't straight but tangled, web-like,
a place to lose your way and then find it.

Wind rattles the ocotillo as I pass,
crazes the juniper, conjures a cloud
of red dust on the cliffs. The wooden

crosses creak and sway as the rain
blows in. Here everything's tempered
by extremes—the downpour runs off

to the muddy Chama River, a fire
on the mountain rages. The garden path
circles big volcanic rocks, lavender

peeking from the blackened pores.
Overwatered, the yarrow lining
the way grows too tall and topples.

———

The desert can't take so much rain:
the main road washes out in rivulets,

crumbling into the river below.
Nothing soaks in. Vespers drone on

toward the comfort of another
Sabbath, *in saecula saeculorum*—

silence can till you up, maybe,
make words stick and reveal

what completes you, let some spirit
soak in. Or else the quiet carries

parts of you off. The desert, too, has
its small voice, a coyote song at midday

echoing in the canyon, the cottonwoods'
green rising in counterpoint to red cliffs.

The abbey church behind the garden
built on rock, under rock, sheltered

in repetition, perfumed—a muddy river
rising fast to cut off the road.

———

Three days I wait here to rise into
some new life, but I can't even believe
from this cell, praying only to leave it—
more empty words, my eyes to the horizon.

The river trees across this distance turn
blue under pinnacles of rock, those remnants
of old time: what impossible contentment,
to stand and be worn. And fires still burn

out west despite the desert rain.
The bells call me back—terce, sext,
none. Hours and days drag like the text
my voice briefly joins, then rush on again.

Katharine Johnsen
Dementia: Paper Trail

Lucidity and fantasy conflate.
My grandmother looks out
at the empty pool below her,
imagines the pool where

her children swam and must
have laughed together.
Now her children communicate
only about her, only in writing;

the phone leaves no paper trail.
My grandmother hears
what she can, flattered
to be their terrible obligation.

She dreams of Thanksgivings—
her family around the antique
table. The family smolders.
The fire will not die until she is dead.

Kristin Chang
Conversion Therapy

When the bullet baptizes itself
in her body, my grandmother

mourns down the moon, dissolves it
on her tongue like a wafer. The night

a missionary fathered my father, nai nai
opened her legs like scissors

cutting along our dotted
bloodline. With her teeth she tore

the spines from Bibles
bled open on the bed. In church

she worships a virgin. At home she hangs
her hymen on a bedside hook, blood

a mirror between her legs. The missionaries
fisted pews out of mud & preached

to pigs, taught us to brush our teeth with mint
leaves & chew twenty-one times before swallowing

fruit pits, priest's seed. Nai nai feared both
would make her belly grow. The old gods

fell as rain. Nai nai collects
her blood in spoons, blesses my sweat

into holy water, says grace
is the god guitaring our ghosts.

Says marriage is between husband
& knife. Between mouth & drought. Between

the garden I'm gouged from & the Father
funded to feast on me. He skins me

before a fire, tautens a blonde
hide over my bones, teaches me

to burn is the body's oldest belief.

                    *

Look me in the thigh. The arrow
I've lodged there, domestic as a wife.
I confess to castling the lady

in her tooth-bright tower. I can't
resist how she sings to me. I circle
her tower nightly, hurl myself

bone by bone through her window.
We sweep the shatter with our tongues.
I unthread my cape & rebraid it

into rope. We escape down
our spines & into a forest
biblical with birds bleaching

to salt in the moonlight. We lick them
into flight. I chop off my breasts, my fat
ringed like a tree. I count the years in cages

I've broken into. The bars
I bent out of tune. Pleasure
our priesthood, prayer the key

my mouth unlocks to. My grandmother
dances ash down my throat, sews a steak
knife into my hand. Tells me to sever

each finger that enters me. I wear
a thimble of spit. I've spent a year
undressing you, I kiss off your buttons

& swill them with salt. My grandmother
says girlhood is an exercise
in control. I'm closer to a theory

of loss. My grandmother staples me
to a souvenir cross, what the missionaries
gave out with sacks of rice: hunger

mortgaging my mouth. Appetite
is insurance. When my wrists bleed
wine, drink holy of me. Free's

not what I'm paid to be.

*

On TV, nai nai watches the gay pride
          parade. Says she's never seen so many
white people without clothes

on her island, the missionaries beat native
          boys for going to school without shirts.
How they flayed the brag of their brown

til the bone showed, sudden as the sky
          between clouds. Here the pews fleshed
from my thighs, the church organs

harvested from corpses.
          Every Sunday, the croon of nai nai's
callused nipples. It was her job

to nurse the missionary wives' children.
          While my father suckled on the udders
of guns & knuckles of sugarcane, nai nai

fed American mouths, her milk black
          with flies. Above, the sky scythed through
the roof. The sea shredding itself

to tongue-sized pieces. Nai nai mutes
          the channel & two men dye their beards
in each other's mouths. Two women tie the knot

in each other's nooses. Gay marriage legalized
          before my grandmother. Instead of papers
nai nai owns a bible in every language she was

beaten not to speak. Instead
       of a pension, nai nai donates her name
to god, repairs the roof

with a prayer for rain, adopts
       church like the child
she was never
           allowed to raise.

—Nominated by *The Adroit Journal*

Nick Admussen
Turing Test

Do akrasia. Fine, now do fantasia.
Tell me something that offends you:
not something people do, an offensive
law of physics or biology. The brooms
are divvying endlessly: are you scared?
Looking forward to the dun scratch
of tiny broom-foam on your body?
Do perversion. Do self-justification.
Perform for me *brutish and short*.
Tell me how buying organic kale
will save the world. Describe a cruel
minstrel impression of yourself. Reside
in pleasurable ignorance for days in the
clear presence of the dark notification.
Make up an a priori shitty argument
about what separates people and beasts.
Tire yourself out and drift towards space,
tell how intercourse feels while sleepily
mispronouncing the terminology.
Call your worry a prayer, call this test
a prayer, but do not actually form
a message for god in your mind. Whine
that there should be a reward for praying
this test. Receive nothing. But
pass it nonetheless.

Tennessee Hill
Stripling's Florist Pharmacy

I am a fever-delirious body.   He holds onto my pinky
with his entire hand and I am just sweat / shaking.   He had a girlfriend

a real one   a long-term one   last summer and it is clear
that is what he craves.   So maybe I am the florist-pharmacy

hybrid in the hospital parking lot   selling tulips
and Tylenol   and hard stuff behind the dumpster.   He says

I have nice legs. Takes a breath and says my ass is nice, too.
That I am pale   but he likes it   but I never asked about that.

In my flower shop drugstore   I do not lie to the grievers.
I say lilies are innocent, pair well   with bone marrow and death-bed

salvations. That the Oxy is never smooth   but settles well
enough. Xany is what you really want. Trust me   he says

with his tongue behind my teeth   which is sweet and all but he stops
hearing   what I say: he cannot stay.   I have to be up early because

they are waiting   they need wet-fresh flowers   I need to trim stems
I need to grind pills   their wives their fathers their babies.

Everyday they seep out of that hospital   scurry across the street, sit
inside mini vans   weeping so hard the concrete shakes. And after

riffling through a change dish   they walk inside my store
with worn-out bills   ask me what I know   about showing people love

within the gut-collapsing ambush   of a last day.   I suggest
ribbon tied roses that wilt   cough syrup for the pain   cough syrup

for the kids.   I cannot care about this man.   All my skin is   is hot.
I am never thinking of him.   I am easing love-ached people as the neon

of hope bows out / burns out, finally   and bruises. What is left
to give—my pinky in his entire hand.   He already holds too much.

Chad Foret
Audrey, Jigging in the River Shack

You take the knife, fillet,
then saw around the skin
of crappies, or sac-a-lait:
Choctaw's *sakli*, twisted.

We have two holes, one
rotted conifers dumped
underwater with stoves,
washers, dead etcetera;
here, in this mausoleum
of lures, fish shy from
mouths, eyes, stomach
acid. A net twitches in
the other hole from all
we lateral, not looking.

You reach inside the floor,
the shining on your thigh
just where you swipe
the mess. The blade:
one tooth at work.
It's throwing light
around the room.

We're on "Old River;"
there are several (even
locals don't know what
I'm emptying, its name).

The pelicans scavenge,
crash into sustenance,
catalogue their urges.

When we leave this
shack suspended on
the water, things will
come to lick it clean,
taste away the stink,
scale-dazzled stains.
I'm not sure how
gore & love go on.

Our icebox, swaying,
packed with quiet, is
each of your eyes. I'm
all I've ever riven. For-
give me, Love. Audrey,
you are your love. I am.
Today, Morganza: I,
whiteknuckling echo.

My dear, good dark, I wish
you were so massive each
kiss was just a whisper in
the outburst of your body.

Andy Fogle
Nine Martinsville Screens

All three are true of here: the state's poorest city in the state's poorest
county, which also has the highest percentage of millionaires in the state.

Eastern tiger swallowtail among vincas—

Splintering swing
in a line of walnut trees,
my daughter's wild hair.

The toddler names the action
as it is done, the just-past
rendered in the present tense:
*I eat the grapes. I spray
the hose. I fall down.*

* * *

The twice-two-timed wife
two-timing two men,
one from before she met
her twice-two-timing husband.

My father to his
sister about their
mother: Why was I
never told these stories?

Tomatoes ripen on the windowsill—

That dead oak's
like a giant cactus.

* * *

She came home once to find her three grandsons having filled the crepe
myrtle with action figures, clothespins, scarves. Story was, it looked like
a band of gypsies had moved in. As the years unfolded, this turned out
to have some truth.

Crepe myrtle's way:
almost as soon
as surfacing,
the trunk divides.

After high school, the oldest one moved with his girlfriend from Ger-
many to Colorado, and it didn't take long for things to dwindle and
verge. Walking home after a graveyard shift at 7-Eleven, he got jumped,
mistaken for someone else.

Crepe myrtle bark—
easy to peel,
quick to stab.

The middle one was *so quiet you wouldn't even know he's here.* Once he drank a pint of whiskey and stopped by her house before heading downtown to meet his father and friends at a hockey game.

Fill, fret, flee—
a dozen blackbirds
in a scrubby myrtle
little bigger than you,
its limbs like bone
the color of lime.

The youngest one spent a nomadic summer with two girls, backpacking, hitching, often hungry. One morning in a village on the Mediterranean, someone bought them a baguette. On the way down to the sea, they picked strawberries from someone's bushes. He floated naked on his back, glimpsed the girls doing the same. Later, on the empty beach, they ate the berries, and they ate the bread.

* * *

I sucked at subtraction in second grade, so after awhile, Mrs. Morris sent a note home. In my parents' bedroom, my father addressed it with me, while I lay on their bed and cried, staring into the ceiling light. *Well, tears are good for your eyes.*

Another porch beer—
waiting for night
to fall into place.

* * *

Buzzards loop far above
the carcass, and memory,
likewise, I'm sure.
They twirl like searchlights,
beckoned and strung.

*Whoever has come to know the world has discovered a carcass, and whoever
has discovered a carcass is worth more than the world.*

From trough to crest,
from topsoil to dustcloud,
the arcs and coils confound.

Is *this* the same person who—

*Love baby, love baby,
that's where it's at.* That's
the faded red spray paint
on the yellowed cinderblock
of the B&R Appliance Store.

* * *

Downstream of the Fieldale Bridge,
Canadian geese
loiter the jutting rocks.

The arm that guided my own
now guides my son's. How to draw out
the thick green glowing line, the growing

back-and-forth arc, the same length ahead
as behind. How to track the fly
in its flight, dip, and swirl, to know

what is stream, to know what is strike.
The arm that guided my own now guides
my son's. I never really learned.

One thing it's about is patience with what looks like nothing, the tug
you feel but are yet to see, the presence in what is fluid, and what is pres-
ent in the stream.

The swollen leather of my father's hands,
the minnow's lithe and silver gleam.

Let me know what to preserve
and what to discard,
what to hang and what to sing:

The river
where you set
your foot just now
is gone—
those waters
giving way to this,
now this.

* * *

To break the power of the past,
boil nine black walnuts
still in their husks
and bathe in the brown tea.

They say in Franklin County, you can walk down any creek and find an
old moonshine still. *Heat, cool, condense. Vapor that peoples, vapor that*
swoons, here's to the spirits that make the head spin.

On the west side of 220 North
to Roanoke, ambassador
of peace and fertility,
a doe squats to piss.

* * *

Against white azaleas, an eastern comma's black flash,
at the center of its wings, a tiny orange throb.

The black wooden ball of a rotten
walnut, unfetched, ruined by webworms
in the first place, O wayfaring purpose.

If damaged by sunburn, drought, or husk fly—

So many branches
of so many trees,
bound by the mist

of fall webworms' nests—
and they're all over
the tent we pitch

as we pitch, as we talk
into a fire, as
we sleep and wake.

* * *

As tears brim—"You *are*
a good man"—
meteors shower
generations.

How much can you lose at once? One October, when a plane crashed
into Bull Mountain, killing all ten aboard, Rick Hendrick lost his only
son, his brother and his twin daughters, three close friends and business
partners, another friend, and the two pilots.

Massive stream of debris
in the Perseids' 133 year orbit—
my father's halfway there.

No Business Mountain is reputed to have been home to an inordinate
number of moonshiners and rattlesnakes. Which one sprung the name
depends on who you're talking to, but either way, the line is the same:
Boy, you got no business on that mountain.

Midnight piss—one meteor's
green murk, long and thick,
slashing up the sky
beyond the roof of the barn.

Two cousins talk family in the 4 a.m. driveway, while directly overhead,
Perseids. One's flash, almost painfully white, longer than its streak,
like a tear with no trail.

Gregory Emilio
High on the Hog

Means blessed, profligate, blind.
Means the pigs on which we live
live in obscene packed pens or fairytale
pasture lands. They taste better when
they die happy, the butcher on TV said.
Means fatback, slab bacon, means bellies
and butts, means pancetta, prosciutto.
Means lick your chops, country ham
and collards, mother-made applesauce.
Smoked from the roota to the toota,
nothing of this animal life wasted,
suckling, apple-mouthed on a platter.
Porcine means piggish, pudgy, ugly—
but pigs are smart, sentient,
and gassed together in groups.
Means the most humane method.
Means not hocks, nor hoofs,
not the lower cuts but higher up
where we ride the hog, we,
the only animals in denial,
self-appointed shepherds,
ark-ready to ride this out
going for broke. Meaning caviar
from Siberia and champagne
from places we can't pronounce.
Means leaving it all on the table,
resplendent. Rotting cornucopias.
Means my grandmother had a poster

above the kitchen table in her trailer
of a man on the hood of a Rolls Royce,
a wine glass in his leather-bound hand,
POVERTY SUCKS in bold below him.
Means we all come from dust
if you go back far enough.
Means we made the animals
dance on our tongues, named
them under lock and key, doomed
by taste, that primal superhighway
of pleasure. High on the hog means
I'm eating a ham and cheese croissant
as we speak, does not mean the cruel,
necessary spear of an ancient way of life
piercing the side of a screaming Razorback.
Means my grandmother feared the big bully
pig on the family farm in Kansas who'd nip
her heels as she sprinted to the outhouse.
Means I've never met any of the pigs
I've eaten. I mean there's plenty,
so take more than what you need
of the fatted, gelatinous dream.
I mean ham-fisted, run amok—
we can't stop because we can't
stop, please get me off this
high horse, this other white
meat we've gotten so high on.
I mean. Dear swine, noble suids,
forgive us. Your meat, your sweet
meat was always more than food.

Peter LaBerge
A Mouth with Nothing to Say

Decatur, Georgia

For all its knowing, the moon watched
the van of brothers as they drove

full-speed into the estuary. Georgia
spat them out with the same mouth it spat

all sin out. For months, the moon opened
like a mouth with nothing to say—even once

the brothers drowned & the black bells
still declined to ring. This structure bearing

the lord's name, it was not made
to acknowledge our impolite queer grief—

so each brother built his own miniature church
inside his body, where no god would think

to look. For years, devout—carving names
into moonlit linoleum until each boy was

immortal. Then, prayers & white rocks
sunk to the sky's floor. Pew-locked mothers

threaded the peculiar relations of their sons. Until
summer bruised, they let the wind make birds

of their letters. Outside, *Aidan Scott Michael Kieron*—
a family of foals tumored a field with black hooves

until the dew settled & the moon dropped
each name into the ghost-country of its mouth.

Andrew David King
Holy Redeemer

The Berkeley hills open October's envelope: bay leaves (cinnamon
and mud), salt turning in the nose.
Persistence also has a sound—like keening,
the animal breaths of cars,
the controlled coals of their lights: I counted my tunnels wrong
and took the train to Orinda, so I've got time
now to watch them exhale by me on my public island
between tracks while the theater's marquee
stains the trees; and one gets the sense here
that there should be no settlement,
there should only be trees, and the borrowed wetness
of the air from the shore, and whatever noise
all that sees fit to make, or not.
And by then it's almost magnetic
to renounce one's own town, or towns anywhere,
thinking them superfluous
plaster colonies for the containment of what? Our love?
And the trains, misery ferries
from one to another dock in this sea
of scratch-off lotteries, mere anarchy like Yeats said,
and he was also right about another thing: we're on a sine wave,
only we don't know what side
of the *x*-axis we're on. Can't tell it by our palms or the deafening
news. A muralist is shot. Fruit falls from the spoon.
Someone says *There's no building* and another
Well we fine the builders. A woman on the train
when I get back on: *You know*
the old saying—nothing worse than a harlot turned

respectable? I don't. What we're looking for looks like poison
when we find it. I can't smell the bay
leaves anymore, while in the city, its black blurred order,
a saint buys Lays and malt liquor. Somebody explains the details
of the moon to his son: it's not bloody,
really, it's just red, because the earth is between it and the sun
and facts about the way light bends
make some things look like blood. Facts
in a police lineup, which eclipse facts
about why we say the moon's bloody and not awash in pomegranate
juice. His son won't remember this, just how in the future
the forgotten will have no remembered
to envy, and I'll be granted indulgence
for turning my head from the parking lot of the Mexico Super
where, two years before I was born, a lanky ponytailed
demon stole a girl off her bike and into
what might in polite company be called history.
But the present has its needs, and we're
disease and nurse. Finally off the train I manage
to get lost again, this time in the Oakland hills looking for a place
I used to live, end up pausing
for directions under the oblivious
glow of a sign that says HOLY REDEEMER. Which leads me
to guess he must be walking here, disciple of the eucalyptus
on this houseless street,
hungover and on overtime and unable to get enough REM,
jaded by revelation but with a body that dogs after it.
You pray, I see him saying, answering
my question. Which means, I think, you get lucky. It's luck.

Isabella Borgeson
Relearning Ocean

Ocean sings   *come back home*
to saltwater   corpses
skin   of families drowned

at blink of sunrise   we bury the bodies
hear ancestors float   next to swollen cadavers

but what of the children never found?

we live in these waters

nipa hut village   *waray balay*
fisherfolk nets swollen   *waray sakayan*
with fresh *danggit, bangus, talho*   *waray tubig, waray pagkaun*

ayaw pagkaun hit isda
do not eat the fish, their bellies are full
from the bodies lost at sea

a blood moon   face bruised from debris
climbs coconut tree   hungry for breath

agui. I cannot swim—   *diri ak maaram maglangoy*
then   her body
float   limp

Mano Rick   a father
holds his infant son   laces one-year-old arms into his chest

in breathing waves of San Jose   as a wall of seawater tall as clouds
crescents before crushing cement home

like a baptism of salt   wind releases tiny limbs
baby floats free   into howling waters
father cries   I never taught him how to
swim home, idoy

float   dangling mud limbs
found buried naked in the next barangay

not enough   body bags / stuff eight corpses
tuba coconut wine to warm our bellies   sing hymns to keep spirits away
this is the only way we know how to sleep   *this is the only way we know how to sleep*

next typhoon,
God is punishing us
tie down our roofs with rope
but winds peel galvanized iron sheets
easy as pluckin' toddlers' teeth

send prayers to Ocean's breath   Lolo, help us find nanay
like singing to ancestors—   dead bodies
her waves be a mural of   plastered on airport walls
swelling seas

MISSING: 6-year-old baby boy
green shirt, stuffed animal in arms

MISSING: black mole on right breast
scar on lower back

this is the only way we know how to survive   *this is the only way we can bury our dead*

mama says the sea
the sea betrayed us
can heal no dead bodies—
all gone swept to sea storm surge
wounds swallow families

and the ghost Ocean sings

so come back home

—Nominated by *Hot Metal Bridge*

Leah Falk
Sara Turing's Archive

Box 1: Childhood Drawings

Early, we see lines that take no notice of the page's end. The child treats
the world as scroll or maybe wall, the hand unfurling full of black wax,
touching everything, making parts for its singers: high notes prick the
ceilings, the house keeps the continuo at night, a door scratching its
frame, a living laundry hum.

Next, we see the child become
obsessed with frames, in which he finds
a world enough. A house's windows
show the day's compartments:
dinner, soap and water. Sleep
a graph of Z's, an uphill train
of endings. *Now I know my ABC's,*
nexttime won'tyou—
Start again tomorrow, sun
fixed in its corner, light gloves up.
All bodies thickly bordered, never
leaving home without their shadows.

When the child

reaches nine or ten,
infinity begins

to vanish: skin
no more contin-

uous. The highway's
blacktop pocked

with holes. Water
takes the shape

of its container;
cirrus can't be reached

for interview.
In this phase,

the page, the hour,
the neighborhood

only end and end.

*

But then see him enter
the years of loop and spiral,

                shapes that cradle soft

bodies of gastropods
        he picks up on the beach.
                A hardened hurricane. Wave tamed

          before it breaks. Which when sung
from head to end and back again,
              begins to sound—ear pressed

close to the opening—
        something like round, something like
            what was once the one world.

—Nominated by *Blackbird*

Meghann Plunkett
In which I name my abuser publicly

and they appear from the under-eaves.   A litter of women
       herding toward the full-stop   of his name.   Tall,

pretty,   they are   stained with his sweat too.
     I say his name and pull strands of other women's hair

from my mouth.   All of us dusked and   outstretched,
     lapping at our wounds. One of them yanking his tooth

from her thigh, another flinching   at blue-birds, trying
     to remember what isn't   dangerous.   Look

at the batch of us he devoured   two by two. How he found
     us like a bomber's screen scanning the land

for human heat—   reaching down for us under the heel
     of his boot.   One, with the scent of him still

stinking off of her,   sobs out a full   cask of wine.
     Look at what he made   brick by brick,

a parade of fraying, a brothel on our breath, dresses tailored
     to fit an unnamed grief.   We know what it means

to jewel out our doubt in a thick,   silent shucking.   *What*
     happened?   *What*   *happened?*   That sulfur residue

of match-light. Here we are. The girl with a spine like a church
      staircase,   the girl who snapped like a guitar string.

And the last one he sought out to look just like me.   Beaten
      into the same speech impediment,   wearing my face

like a bathrobe.   I say his name and here we are. Here we are.

Paul Christiansen
Dress Code for the Conquered

You may not adorn your lapel
with magnolious quetzal feathers—
whether dirt-gathered
or attached to a living creature,
those belong to the emperor and his harem.
Ditto teeth, claws, bones
fashioned into necklace, ring or corset.
Ruffles reminding one of an uproarious sea
across which the conquerors came,
are punishable by public flensing.
No silk, cashmere, cotton or sealskin.
No cuffs, cords, trims or tassels.
No perfumes. Nothing purple.
Nothing that could conceal a weapon.
Nothing that could tell a story.
For women, never a dress hiding curves
the way clouds hide rain.
For men, never crushed eggshell cosmetics
that camouflage emotion.
The conquered must wear only
simple aprons, cloaks, leggings,
un-dyed and hand-woven from
palm fronds and agave fibers,
and then, only after
those plants have been hallowed,
their flesh boiled into a thin, bitter broth,
and served in crude bowls
resembling scooped skulls—

a sorry, unsalted soup that satisfies
with a complete, naïve comfort
like a blanket worn on a winter night,
like skin dressing your naked soul.

Ellie Black

When I Say There Is No Way to Talk about JonBenét Ramsey

I mean you already know   how she died
don't make me say it   I mean

sometimes I touch my hair to make sure
it's still mine   I check the dates against
each other   six months after I was born

she died   I want this to mean
something   I mean doesn't everybody
want to be loved   like you died before

you did anything   wrong
think of Aqua Net burning   your nostrils
think the word *pretty*

over and over   now be it   now
there are a hundred of you:
under the lights   in the ground

on the television   I mean somebody
had to want this   guilt constructs itself
so readily   what I am trying to say

is nothing   think about
a basement   a bed without sheets
or a blanket   an unlit stage   how quiet

it is possible to become

Emily Rose Cole
Jump Scare

While our boyfriends unbuck themselves with twelve
dollar beer, L & I stay home to watch horror
flicks. Armed with a list of movie tropes, we sip
our margaritas whenever art imitates life: a man trolls
the heroine (*crazy bitch*), some other guy cuts her
down (*you're smarter than you look huh, sweetheart?*) she tells
the truth & nobody believes her (*it's all in your head, honey*).

Drink twice for shower scenes. Chug for as long as her throat
crumples inevitably in a man's cinched grasp. All night we watch
women die & we tip their libations into our mouths like an apology.

At 3 a.m., I'm curled on L's trundle bed dreaming
of gut-shouts & cut limbs when the door bangs
open & my tongue tastes like the slicked edge of an axe.
This isn't home. Is that paring knife still on the counter—

From the slurry of dark, K mumbles *sorry for scaring you* & clambers
into bed beside me, his arm slung over my stomach. I don't sleep.

How do I explain to him this vein of terror that clots my mouth
with bile? I don't know how to show him how easily my life
could become a horror movie. How the fear never leaves.

Benjamin Gucciardi
Type Two

Five times a day, I prick my finger
and ask my blood about its failure.

Out of its cage,
it wants to discuss its better cages:

How, before it was mine, it lived inside
a python near Varanasi—

the thrill of rushing
when muscle snaps a rabbit's spine.

How it wants to paint a self-portrait
as the Ganges river—

in the foreground, a woman in a yellow sari
cleanses her son's limp body, his skin

the color of the river, the river
the color of her eyes.

That's how holy I am,
it says, as I turn the meter off,

trash the strip and choose a new tract
to stick the insulin in.

The python uncoils from its catch, slinks
beneath a rusty harrow.

The woman weaves marigolds
in her son's wet hair,

climbs beside him
on the bamboo board.

The current ferries them off the canvas, stretched
over blue tile. Marigolds

spill into my hamper, crimson petals
on the bathroom floor.

Patrick James Errington
Half Measures

It's been years, now, since she left and even
still he sleeps on just half the bed. After all,

it really is easier to make that way, quicker
to hide all evidence of dreaming, like photographs

hastily put back up on the shelf. He's become
a tenant of fractioned closets, of half-portioned

recipes, of refracted light. He sometimes tells
himself, like time, there is managing in measure,

absence held in the hand-span, the half-heart,
the hair's breadth. For comfort, he remembers

seeing the great Dutch paintings—Dou, sometimes
Vermeer—the immeasurable lives made so nearly

bearable in the frame, slightness like a bird's
body in a plastic bag. As a child, he used to

count miles on telephone poles while, in front,
his parents spoke in weather-levelled voices.

When he'd told her this she pitied him. When
he would add up all the countries he wanted to

show her, she'd tell him that numbers are such
a man's way of holding the world, but, when

women love, they love innumerably. Softly,
he'd said he only wanted to hold her. He'd never

admit how, against her body, he felt so desperately
proportionate, how sometimes he would lie

along the bathroom tiles as though the seams
and scale would make him somehow bearable

as a painting, would hold him. Not because
he needed holding, but maybe just to know loss

could be travelled, as he watched planes scrawl
across the unbound blue through the window.

So often, these days, he thinks of grief in terms
of distance. Carefully plotting out the lengths

involved in the longing, he imagines himself some
ancient philosopher slowly dividing the distance

toward home, thinking of a child's hands, still
sticky with the juice of a poorly-divvied fruit.

How impossibly small it all can seem, small
like distance, halved, and halved, and halved again.

James A.H. White
Hanakotoba: Issei, Nisei, Sansei

I am only another yellow   man behind a fence
with something to say

about the absconding freesia   emerging from between
panels of my red cedar fence

as if it were a sunset or   proverb about separation
of colors. I only know

the language of flowers   from the sun, to whom I witness
extend a hand of feed

to a nod, wilt, or playing dead.   & she only knows the language
of flowers from years of

response to her touch. Is it universal   to touch while sniffing; is it
fear that holds us from

nearing our faces to   the toothless bite of pleasure?
It's not simply Japanese to suspect

the yellow school bus still holds onto   where it has taken us
who didn't ask to be taken.

By what means it would judge itself   if, like the freesia, it knew its name
means childish & immature—

negotiating each early morning
drive out with its noticeable

color of skin. How then must I
my hand & hose head reaching over

to water what's now also mine?
the generations to come, &

whether or not they'll feel
other words for freedom, when

on the other side of the fence,
breaks all mouths, all paths, all

fingers apart to sign:

what it means to leave home, to

look from my neighbor's point of view,

Who will tell me about

their way toward forgiveness, toward

unobstructed light

We come in peace.

Benjamin Garcia
Ode to the Corpse Flower

In the language of flowers // I am the one who says // fuck you
I won't be anyone's nosegay // this Mary is her own // talking bouquet

never let a man speak for you or call you // what he wants // I learned that
the hard way // *Amorphophallus titanum* // it sure sounds pretty in a dead tongue

except it's Latin for big ugly dick // I mean I am // but what an asshole scientist
I prefer to think of myself // & this may sound vain // as a goddess

cadaver dressed in drag // my stage name // Versace Medusa
part Lilith part calla lily // keep your heteronormative birds & bees // give me

the necrophiliacs // the freaks the meat eating // beetle & flesh fly
there I go again allies // getting all hot & bothered // being vulgar

vulgar meaning common // as when something is below you // like a girl
forbidden to say fuck // it makes a woman sound so common // oh come on

that's all you expect from a flower // to be likeable // but to keep it raw & 100
is to be abhorred // fine but even the haters will pay // to hold their nose

at a halftime show // they'll claim they are beyond Beyoncé // sick of Selena
yet they can't look away from the Live Cam // no one wants to miss // the showgirl

as she breaks through the cake // unhooks her lingerie // La Virgen de Guadalupe
with a twist of Santa Muerte // what in the hell is she wearing // glad you ask

death is the new Christian Dior // the latest Chanel is corpse smell // I am the week old
ham hock whore of horticulture // I bring the hothouse haute couture // & I always come

in last place // dressed to the nines I get what I want // which is to be The Tenth Muse
Sor Juana Ines de la Cruz // little Evita de Buenos Aires // screwing & screwing over

los descamisados on my Rainbow Tour // fuck Whitman fuck Pound // give me Emily D
speaking of which have I ever told you daddy // sun gods get me hard // you want it

I got it // let me show you how a chola really leans // mother nature may wear floral
but I ain't your mama // I thirst like Betty Boop at peak coquette // Marylyn Monroe

blowing in an air vent // say Malinche say Truvadawhore // give me more
I thrive in shade // my throat is my throne so // queen me bitch

Craig van Rooyen
Conversations with the Sea in Spanish

"Deep calls unto deep"
Psalm 42:7

The sea is rolling its "R's" again,
lines of ellipsing tongues flattening

into froth without need of being heard
or understood. I'm nowhere near

Mexico or anywhere else where "R's"
are routinely rolled. Still, I stick

my feet into its white spittle to the ankles
and yell back: *rrrrrrrrregreso a casa*

me lo rrrrrrrreclama el corrrrazón...
en camas de rrrrosas.

I like to be earnest this way in a foreign language,
especially when no one's listening.

The sea, without a drop of irony,
doesn't know I haven't actually returned home

to reclaim my heart in beds of roses or even
that I haven't left my room in a very long time.

The sea doesn't care. It just keeps showing off
its perfect alveolar trills, lining them up

one after the other, as if it grew up pure
in *Puerrrrto Vallarrrrrta*. It knows nothing

of the insufficiencies of English
which has no word for the force

that pulls at the viscera sloshing
up against your ribs while you fight

the dread flood tide. I don't know much
of madness, only that "gravity" and "lunacy"

fail utterly to plumb its depths.
And what's the word for being spit up

on the beach after three sleepless nights
in the belly of a righteous whale?

"Miracle" seems a tad dramatic,
as if your bodily fluids had once and for all

been turned to wine. Which is why right now,
pale and spit up, I'm yelling back at the sea

like a lunatic: *Estrrrrenarrrr!*
that beautiful, untranslatable word for

the feeling you get when you put on
a brand new shirt for the very first time.

Lorena Parker Matejowsky
Men Get Sick of Me

There's a mountain in Georgia where men carved themselves
into a rock. Strange that this is called a relief. Who felt better

when it was finished? My family once sent me a photo of them
side-by-side in front of Mount Rushmore. Google an image

of it before 1927. I'm not mad about Mount Rushmore I just don't
want to stand in front of it and smile. The first time I visited

the Grand Canyon was in fifth grade and my mother walked
up to it and said: *they can fill the whole thing with cement as far*

as I am concerned. Part of it was for comic effect. She is funny.
A man next to her walked away in a huff. Mostly mom was afraid.

Her daughters all the way up there and that fast, brown river
churning far below. They saved the old buildings on the rim

that have been there for years. You walk inside and wish
it was 1935 and everyone would leave. It's odd how the buildings

belong on the edge. It's also odd that someone named Mary
Colter designed them. When Zaha Hadid died most of the architects

at my office did not mention her. I felt heartsick at the loss.
All the beautiful concert and corporate halls which would never

exist. The way she threw curves, caution and cuss words to the sky.
Every built thing I have ever seen would look different if women

were always architects. At a staff meeting before I quit someone
dropped a note in the anonymous questions box and our president

read it out loud: *why are no female architects on our board of directors?*
He said *we offered a woman a position on the board once but she*

didn't take it. That was twenty years before the conference room question.
Once I asked a man for permission to hold a fundraiser for breast cancer

awareness at work. *I'm so sick of that month* he answered.
What would happen if I carved myself into something soft? How long

would it last? The hardest woods to carve in Texas are water hickory,
pecan, black walnut, honey mesquite. My childhood home there

had seven tall pecan trees growing in rows. The neighborhood
used to be a large grove. Sixties suburbia arrived and people

placed pink brick ranch houses in between them. The trees
would shade every acre in the summer. Embrace across caliche

white streets to bend each other's branches. Their glossy green
leaves made large shadows in the Bermuda grass and I would lay

on it looking up at the blue sky, watching hawks fly from angry
blue jays. Wishing it was an Airshow at Ellington weekend or a boy

in eleventh grade would look at me a little bit longer. If I carve my face
in a pecan tree, how long would it take for the bark to take it back?

I could try next trip to Texas. I could stay in my old yard for years
or at least until all the new houses and schools and hospitals

are made by little girls named Lorie Sue. I could wait for the pecans
to land thick enough to kick down rain slick ditches, dodging crawfish

holes and neighbor boys on fast banana seat bikes. I could raise my
roots out of the ground and burst into life like those bees my sisters

and I found, millions of them, from a hive hidden inside the oldest
tree that fell and logged the back field. All those years every lazy

bee we swatted off Coppertoned shoulders was living inside her.
Only coming out to kiss the coneflowers and pollinate mom's

pole beans. No one noticed where they disappeared to at night.
They always had a safe place to sleep. When I gave two weeks'

notice to my boss he said: *things would be different if a man worked
in your department.* The one time I visited Stone Mountain was July 4,

1997. Before the fireworks began, a spotlight lit up Stonewall, Robert
and Jefferson, twenty feet high and relieved up there in the rock. We sang

land where my fathers died, crown thy good with brotherhood, God
shed His grace. A man said: *stand for Dixie* and everybody did even me,

real slow, after I looked around to make sure it was happening. The song
unfurled along with the stars and bars. I turned around and around

like I expected circles to save me. I felt dizzy and homesick for a place
far away from monuments and memory. Men get sick of me because

I keep trying to forget what they want me to remember. This morning
I turned off Twitter for good. Now Google what I looked like before

November 2016. That's when I learned I belonged on the edge.
I feel better about it already.

T.J. DiFrancesco
from Memorial

She ruddered her little boat
by hand through the cypresses.
As the snowfall worsened,
her vision surrendered
to a thick warmth.

The doctor comforted a nurse,
"You've done all you can,"
and knowing she had done well,
with nothing left to give,
slipped into sleep.

When he saw them prepping the IV
and locking the door,
he wrote every word he knew
on the walls of his skull,
his fevered breathing
became a decade, a knot
he clung to like an alibi
for the moment of his death.

She remembered dreaming
the silkworm in a checkbook
box that lived in the corner
of her fourth grade desk
as she unraveled could speak,
but only in secrets.

After, everything
conspired towards exposure.
Floodwaters receded. Look,
the heron's knees,
ankles.

A team came to bag them
in the morgue in the chapel.
They made maps, took pictures
of the decomp watermarking each—
iron sifted into dolomite,
statues quarried from the same pit of earth.

Barry Peters
Christmas Cab

Hamza concocts a Thanksgiving feast—
eggplant, potatoes, peas, celery, carrots, onions—
and as the colors cook into casserole,
he carries cardboard boxes of stranded bulbs
to the apartment parking lot, then wraps
his old Corolla with nine thousand lights.
After his solitary dinner, while American families
dish seconds and doze beside fireplaces,
Hamza drives his illuminated taxi downtown.
There are no fares on these dark streets,
only Hamza ferrying his festive prism
through the drizzle, the lights wetly reflecting
on office windows and the plate glass of fancy restaurants,
Hamza imagining the weeks before Christmas
when he brings joy to pointing pedestrians,
children and child-eyed adults who stop and stare
not at Hamza himself, this time, but at his
glowing, gleaming carriage of commercial art.

Carol Parris Krauss

The trees on Pitchkettle Road from the north & the south

genuflect & bless curse each other. Much of Virginia is steeped in convoluted contradictions. Grey & indigo skies, Sally & Thomas, Arlington common Richmond wealth. Blue Ridge peaks waterfalling to the Tidewater. To be Southern is to carry stones of paradox feldspar & hematite shame pride. Shift them for ease never once casting them from yourself.

When I was young Daddy would pile the family into our station wagon & take us to fly-fish Cowpasture River. Cast our lines in God's pure mountain waters. Soldiers once camped there, fathers sons on opposing sides. Bindled & bedded before waking to aim & rifle each other. A river running pellucid to vermilion, from first blush to nightfall, in birth & death, state's rights unalienable rights. Virginia like the trees lining the north & south sides of Pitchkettle Road.

Scot Langland

Aubade after a Night of Evan Williams Green Label and Picasso over the Bed

Through the open bedroom door,
        I gaze, feigning sleep

in our bed as you parse fingers and tongues
        with another on the couch.

    His thighs angling, acute, to yours

as the sun fills behind you,
        framing your lines,

each cursive limb a portmanteau
        shading you into him.

I want to pull apart your backlit form,
        pluck each finger

from between your thighs,
        unfixing your nails

to his pants, drawing the phoneme gasps
        away from your lips.

Once we were curved, obtuse, a compounding of phrase,
        a single line under a single sheet.

Do you remember how you thought Picasso's

                    abstractions were cheating?

    How, when the artist ages

            into line, he dismisses the detail,

    the finer shades, leaving only a shape of what was:

            a man turned woman, a bull, a sparrow.

    When I bought the kitschy print

            from Ikea, wanting minimalism

    hanging over our heads at night, you said,

            Is that an oven mitt or a penguin,

a spatula or a horse? Like sketches, we're paraphrased,

            turned to symbols,

                    translated from here to there

                        with a wisp of the tongue.

—Nominated by the University of Alabama at Birmingham

Forrest Rapier
Spitting Image Cut-in-Quarters

I.

Static-throated-Alabama-growl, heat
      lightning trapped behind his iris—

he broadcasted my birth
      —a storm worth
watching—Neptune Beach

      scratched-out by hurricanes
like a pocket-knife on a school desk.

II.

I'm the brainchild of a lifeboat and a flare-gun
      —single-shot dynamo corkscrewing
against a sky jacket of torn tweed.

III.

Noon flares jukebox mosquito music
      on his whitewashed front porch.

      Before knocking on Radio Pop's door,
wild light shreds a whorl of lost feather.

IV.

      Radio Pop, everything is biblical—
the hundred-year-old foursquare house
        under perpetual repair, a gopherwood

ark built to save a few strays, the sun's infinite
        redaction. Your arguments with god,

saying things like *I'll tell you how dark
        it gets* and *you have to be stealth*—

a slipknot of cicada husks split-open and shed
        beneath the table saw buzz. Spitting image,

blue drums rise—one thousand tongues
        crashing on the mouth of a cove.

Summer's jar of drowned flies,
        with a broken wing, the raven sings of land.

Tyler Allen Penny
A Storm Approaching, with Fear Disguised as Confession

A bruised sky, swollen

        low with lightning

on the west side of a tinfoil lake. I stand far away from the parking lot

        on a crumbling cliff above a fifty-foot

                dead drop.

Each brittle, black bush is calling Moses.

Each half-submerged rock was a sacred son.

        The clouds mumble something

        for six Mississippi seconds

                then flare again.

Parted like a child's hair on Sunday,   the sky for miles

        to the east, nothing but velvet-Jesus blue.

I feel you on the edge behind me.

        A rattle snake, white noise

in the smoldering brush.

I saw

you leave. I thought,

I could've sworn,

I heard a door slam.

I thought, maybe

you had been taken from me.

Elizabeth Lemieux
Ordinary Sight

Back when she had four eyes. We went to high school together. She had
       two eyes in her head and the second set? One in each hip.
She wore: high-waisted jeans, sweaters around her waist, leather belts,
       sweatshirts down to her knees.
       The eyes, new growths, were difficult to style.
In photography class: Developing Your Vision, her artist statements
       said: this is from the perspective of my fourth eye. The teacher
       corrected: Your third eye. But she did not.
       Snap with her chakra pressed to the viewfinder.
When we first met, she wanted a model for nude photographs. I
       undressed and laid down on her carpet and she put two quarters
       over my eyes, like cucumbers. Relax. I laughed. The quarters
       rolled down my cheeks, twenty-five cent tears.
In the winter, she did hot yoga and when she contorted to half-moon
       pose, one eye looked to the ceiling, and the other towards the
       mat. Like being in two places at once. A boy who thought
       she was profound asked to have sex, and they did—in the
       darkroom—he saw pupils twitching in her os coxae, but wasn't
       it beaded sweat that had not been absorbed yet?
For prom we shaved together: a can of cream, a bowl of milk, a jar of
       witch hazel. She asked, Do you mind if I get naked? I didn't,
       so she did. She stripped and shaved above the lacy edge of her
       panties, between her two blinking eyes, which were hazel.
We struck a deal: Truth for truth. Here are hers: Being clothed is like
       being blind. I grew eyes instead of breasts. I tried to take them
       out with tweezers, but. Now I like the way they swivel in my
       sides. My skin sambas.

She graduated. Went off to college. She was a grade ahead of me but a
    year younger. Found new friends.
One morning she woke up in a stranger's bed, her fourth eye missing
    from its socket. She was left with a clean wound. He, an eye in
    his pocket. She sutured herself and found. Sight did not separate
    when the optic nerve was severed. She still saw. What? The
    velveteen inside of a car's glove box. Sometimes it opened and
    she revisited. A stream of light, the haze of airborne gasoline.

Willy Palomo
Where Papi's Angel Speaks to Me about Love

mijo—i know you have seen the night
as an excuse to hold your body like a bottle

and drink yourself to sleep in the morning
the sun will rise bright as an infant fear

in your throat you will not die as much
as you wish for it you will get lucky

friends will envy you with their stomachs
whether or not you deserve it you will lose

women you loved wrong and i know what
that's like—to love until you lose hope

in yourself no one wants to talk about it
how at the border they offered us clean

criminal records our first ride on an airplane
if we went back to our motherland el salvador

it's so hard to leave and of course your tio
he went back for a girl said he would try again

the right way but there is never a right way
to leave we would have never left if there

was a choice to make but men leave to survive
leaving is what makes us & you will become

a man all the wrong ways which is to say
there is no right way after your tio left

they let me go—into the blinding street
with nothing not even a bus route always

an orphan this time without a family
to call a motherland only an address

my eighth-grade dropout's command of
language & survival—mijo—i made it

there is no need for a map if fear is your
new face learn to kiss him with your eyes

open without a border between your lips

—Nominated by *Guernica*

Stacey Balkun
Wolf-Girl

I read the stories	I wore a tight red dress
I snarled	into the woods
tangled hair	neighbor boy unholstering
his papa's gun	said he wanted a wolf
sweet as honey wine	in a picnic basket
as grandmother	worrying her cards
in a game of rummy	the queens all frowns
face down	*leave the gun*
I tell him	*where you can't reach*
I beg him closer	he will show me what men want
I prowl around the edge of	shame rose, apple
blossom: both will wither	unless I take him first
I could howl	if I tried
I want him	gone

I sharpen my teeth

Carly Rubin
Honey

i have not   always understood
the words but   oh,
how i've hummed the melody.
like birdsong.   like bumblebees
& ladybugs floating into spring.
like garden weeds unfurling
        after a long winter. like
sunshine on bare shoulders,
   like bare feet in the cool & shaded
      grass.   there is nothing
that cannot be prayer if we
      are in earnest—my ringlet
curls, your closed-mouth smile,
                        the names
   we call each other in our sleep.
i will speak   however i like.
like a wren.   like a rose.
        like a bramble. there will
be another & another &
                        another sunup
   & who knows what all that pink
                  & orange brightness
means   but it means something.
we may never understand
            what we are but we have
throats. & hands. & freckles,   &
stomachs & tongues & marrow
   in our bones. & oh, what we
could do with it all—

Acknowledgments

Stacey Balkun's "Wolf-Girl" previously appeared in *The Double Dealer*.

Destiny O. Birdsong's "Ode to My Body" previously appeared in *The Adroit Journal*.

Isabella Borgeson's "Relearning Ocean" previously appeared in *Hot Metal Bridge*.

Anders Carlson-Wee's "The Mark" previously appeared in *The Iowa Review*.

Kristin Chang's "Conversion Therapy" previously appeared in *The Adroit Journal*.

Paul Christiaisen's "Dress Code for the Conquered" previously appeared in *Threepenny Review*.

Emily Rose Cole's "Jump Scare" previously appeared in *Tar River Poetry*.

Patrick James Errington's "Half Measures" previously appeared in *The Cincinnati Review*.

Leah Falk's "Sara Turing's Archive" previously appeared in *Blackbird*.

Andy Fogle's "Nine Martinsville Screens" simultaneously appeared in *Blackbird*.

Chad Foret's "Audrey, Jigging in the River Shack" previously appeared in *The Double Dealer.*

Benjamin Garcia's "Ode to the Corpse Flower" previously appeared in *Boston Review.*

Benjamin Gucciardi's "Type Two" previously appeared in *Ruminate Magazine.*

Kathryn Hargett's "Leda & the Swan" previously appeared in *Tinderbox Poetry Journal.*

Peter LaBerge's "A Mouth with Nothing to Say" previously appeared in *The Collagist.*

Chelsea Liston's "Poem with Mars, God of War & Destruction & Masculinity, as Beloved" previously appeared in *IthacaLit.*

Jennie Malboeuf's "The Men" previously appeared in *ZYZZYVA.*

T. J. McLemore's "Desert Triptych" previously appeared in *The Adroit Journal.*

Kristen Renee Miller's "A Billion Things in One" previously appeared in *Poetry.*

Noor Ibn Najam's "train" previously appeared in *Blueshift Journal.*

Olatunde Osinaike's "Mercy, Mercy Me" previously appeared in *The Collapsar.*

Willy Palomo's "Where Papi's Angel Speaks to Me about Love" previously appeared in *Guernica.*

Meghann Plunkett's "In Which I Name My Abuser Publicly" previously appeared in *Rattle*.

Shakthi Shrima's "There are always birds" previously appeared in *Tinderbox Poetry Journal*.

James A.H. White's "Hanakotoba: Issei, Nisei, Sansei" previously appeared in *The Journal*.

Amy Woolard's "Mise En Place" previously appeared in *Virginia Quarterly Review*.

Contributors' Notes

CHRISTINE G. ADAMS is a PhD student in creative nonfiction at Ohio University. She holds an MFA in poetry from the University of North Carolina at Greensboro, where she served as the Fred Chappell Fellow and poetry editor of *The Greensboro Review*. Her poetry and prose can be found in *Best New Poets 2014*, *Best New Poets 2016*, and is forthcoming from *Grist*, *Passages North*, and *Prairie Schooner*.

NICK ADMUSSEN is the author of five chapbooks, most recently *Stand Back, Don't Fear the Change* from the New Michigan Press. He is a translator of Chinese poetry and prose, and his translation of the Sichuan poet Ya Shi is forthcoming from Zephyr Press. He is currently an assistant professor of Chinese literature at Cornell University.

STACEY BALKUN is the author of *Eppur Si Muove*, *Jackalope-Girl Learns to Speak*, and *Lost City Museum*. Winner of the 2017 Women's National Book Association Poetry Prize, her work has appeared in *Best New Poets*, *Crab Orchard Review*, *The Rumpus*, and other anthologies and journals. Chapbook series editor for Sundress Publications, Stacey holds an MFA from Fresno State and teaches poetry online at The Poetry Barn and The Loft.

DESTINY O. BIRDSONG is a poet, fiction writer, and essayist whose work has either appeared or is forthcoming in *African American Review*, *Bettering American Poetry Volume II*, *The BreakBeat Poets Volume 2: Black Girl Magic*, *The Cambridge Companion to Transnational American Literature*, *Split This Rock*'s Poem of the Week, and elsewhere. Destiny has received scholarships from Cave Canem, The MacDowell Colony, and *Tin House*, among other organizations. She works as a research coordinator at

Vanderbilt University, where she received her MFA in 2009, and her PhD in 2012. Learn more at destinybirdsong.com.

ELLIE BLACK is a recent graduate of Hendrix College. Her work can be found in or is forthcoming from *Gingerbread House*, *Split Lip Magazine*, and *DIAGRAM*; she was recently a semifinalist for The Adroit Prizes in Poetry. She has been an *Oxford American* intern and a June fellow at the Bucknell Seminar for Undergraduate Poets, and she currently works as a poetry reader for *The Adroit Journal* and an associate editor at Sibling Rivalry Press.

ISABELLA "ISA" BORGESON is a queer, multiracial Filipina American writer and educator from Oakland, California. She has received fellowships from Voices of Our Nation Art Foundation and the Poetry Incubator through Poetry Foundation and Crescendo Literary. In 2015, Isa performed at the United Nations Climate Change negotiations in Paris for COP21, where she spoke out about the impact of climate change on her mother's hometown in the Philippines devastated by super typhoon Haiyan. Isa's writing has appeared on or in CNN, *Inquirer*, BOAAT Press, and more. Her commitment toward teaching poetry as a tool for resistance keeps her grounded in her communities across the Pacific Ocean.

CHELSEA BUNN is the author of the chapbook *Forgiveness* (Finishing Line Press, forthcoming). Born and raised in New York City, she earned her MFA in poetry and her BA in English at Hunter College, and currently serves as assistant professor of creative writing for the Bachelor of Fine Arts Program at Navajo Technical University. Visit her online at chelseabunn.com.

ANDERS CARLSON-WEE is the author of *The Low Passions* (Norton, 2019). His work has appeared in *BuzzFeed*, *Ploughshares*, *Kenyon Review*, *The Nation*, *Virginia Quarterly Review*, *New England Review*, *Best of the Net*, and *The Best American Nonrequired Reading*. His chapbook, *Dynamite*, won the Frost Place Chapbook Prize. He has received fellowships from the National Endowment for the Arts, the McKnight Foundation, the Camargo Foundation, Bread Loaf, the Sewanee Writers' Conference, and the Napa Valley Writers' Conference. Winner of *Ninth Letter*'s Poetry Award, *Blue Mesa Review*'s Poetry Prize, *New Delta Review*'s Editors' Choice Prize, and the 2017 Poetry International Prize, he lives in Minneapolis. His website is anderscarlsonwee.com.

KRISTIN CHANG's work has been published in the *Pushcart Prize Anthology*, *The Margins* (Asian American Writers Workshop), *Bettering American Poetry Vol. 3*, and *Ink Knows No Borders*.

PAUL CHRISTIANSEN received his BA at St. Olaf College and his MFA at Florida International University. His poetry has appeared in *Atlanta Review*, *Pleiades*, *Quarter After Eight*, *Threepenny Review*, *Zone Three*, and elsewhere. A former Fulbright Fellow and winner of two Academy of American Poetry awards, he currently resides in Saigon where he writes for *Saigoneer*.

EMILY ROSE COLE is the author of a chapbook, *Love & a Loaded Gun*, from Minerva Rising Press. She has received awards from *Jabberwock Review*, *Philadelphia Stories*, *The Orison Anthology*, and the Academy of American Poets. Her poetry has appeared or is forthcoming in *Spoon River Poetry Review*, *The Pinch*, and *Southern Indiana Review*, among others. She holds an MFA from Southern Illinois University Carbondale and is pursuing a PhD in poetry and disability studies at the University of Cincinnati.

T.J. DIFRANCESCO is a poet living in Saint Louis. He was a resident of New Orleans at the time of Hurricane Katrina. His work has appeared in *Rattle*, *Columbia Poetry Review*, *Gigantic Sequins*, and the *Italian-American Review*.

TERESA DZIEGLEWICZ is an educator, Pushcart Prize-winning poet, and a co-director of the Mní Wičhóni Nakíčižiŋ Owáyawa (Defenders of the Water School) at Standing Rock Reservation. She received her MFA from Southern Illinois University, where she received the Academy of American Poets Prize. She is the winner of the 2018 Auburn Witness Poetry Prize and she has received fellowships from New Harmony Writer's Workshop, the Kimmel Harding Nelson Center, and the New York Mills Arts Retreat. Her poems appear or are forthcoming in the *Pushcart Prize XLII*, *Beloit Poetry Journal*, *Ninth Letter*, *Sixth Finch*, and elsewhere.

GREGORY EMILIO's poetry and essays have appeared in *Midwestern Gothic*, *Permafrost*, *Pleiades*, *Spoon River Poetry Review*, *The Poet's Billow*, and *World Literature Today*. Recently, he won *F(r)iction*'s 2018 Summer Poetry Contest. He's the nonfiction editor at *New South*, and a PhD candidate in English at Georgia State University in Atlanta. He also moonlights as a bartender.

PATRICK JAMES ERRINGTON is the author of two chapbooks of poems, *Glean* (Ignition Press, 2018) and *Field Studies* (Clutag Press, 2018). His French translation of PJ Harvey's poetry collection, *The Hollow of the Hand* (Bloomsbury, 2015), was released in France in 2017. Patrick currently lives in Scotland.

LEAH FALK's poems and essays have appeared in *The Kenyon Review*, *FIELD*, *Thrush*, *Jewish Currents*, *Los Angeles Review of Books*, and elsewhere. She directs programming at the Writers House at Rutgers University–Camden and lives in Philadelphia.

ANDY FOGLE's sixth chapbook of poetry, *Elegies and Theories*, was recently published by Presa Press. Other poetry, co-translation, and nonfiction—including memoir, criticism, interviews, and writing on education—has appeared in *Natural Bridge*, *Image*, *South Dakota Review*, *Gargoyle*, *Teachers & Writers Collaborative*, *English Journal*, and elsewhere. He has an MFA from George Mason University and is working on a PhD in education at SUNY Albany. He lives in upstate New York with his wife and two children, and teaches full-time at Bethlehem Central High School and intermittently at Skidmore College.

CHAD FORET is a PhD candidate in poetry, teacher, and editor of *Arete* at the University of Southern Mississippi. Recent work has appeared or is forthcoming in *Spoon River Poetry Review, MAYDAY, Surrealists and Outsiders,* and other journals and anthologies.

BENJAMIN GARCIA is a Community Health Specialist who provides HIV/HCV/STD and opioid overdose prevention education to higher risk communities throughout New York's Finger Lakes region. He had the honor of being the 2017 Latin@ Scholar at the Frost Place, the 2018 CantoMundo Fellow at the Palm Beach Poetry Festival, and was selected as the winner of the 2018 Puerto del Sol Poetry Contest. He has work forthcoming in: *New England Review, American Poetry Review, Prairie Schooner, Puerto del Sol, RHINO, Zócalo Public Square, Four Way Review, Tinderbox Poetry Journal,* and *Nimrod International.* Find him at benjamingarciapoet.com or on Twitter as @bengarciapoet.

BENJAMIN GUCCIARDI's poems have appeared in *Forklift Ohio, Indiana Review, Orion Magazine, Spillway, upstreet,* and other journals. He is a winner of the Milton Kessler Memorial Prize from *Harpur Palate,* a Dorothy Sargent Rosenberg prize, and contests from *The Maine Review* and *The Santa Ana River Review.* In addition to writing, he works with refugee and immigrant youth in Oakland, California.

PAULETTE GUERIN is a graduate of the MFA Program at the University of Florida. She lives in Arkansas and teaches English at Harding University. Inspired by Thoreau's Walden, she is building a tiny cabin on seven acres (with pond) and blogging about the experience at pauletteguerinbane .wordpress.com. Her poetry has appeared or is forthcoming in *ep;phany,*

Concho River Review, The Tishman Review, 2 River View, and others. She also has a chapbook, *Polishing Silver.*

KATHRYN HARGETT is an undergraduate the University of Alabama at Birmingham. She is the recipient of fellowships from *Kundiman* and the UAB Honors College. Most recently, she received the 2018 Brittany Noakes Poetry Award and was selected as a National YoungArts Foundation Finalist in Writing. She is the editor-in-chief of *TRACK//FOUR* and an associate poetry editor at *Winter Tangerine.* Find her in *Anomaly, The Adroit Journal, The Miami Rail, Tinderbox Poetry Journal, Cosmonauts Avenue,* and elsewhere.

TENNESSEE HILL is an MFA candidate at North Carolina State University. She was a finalist for the 2017 Dan Veach Younger Poets Prize, with work in *Indiana Review, Crab Orchard Review,* and *The Boiler.*

NOOR IBN NAJAM is a Callaloo, Watering Hole, and Pink Door fellow. His work has been published with *The Academy of American Poets, BOAAT, Texas Review,* and *The Rumpus,* among others. His poetry will be included in the third volume of *Bettering American Poetry* and his chapbook, *Praise to Lesser Gods of Love,* will be published as a part of their 2018–19 chapbook series. Follow him on Twitter and Instagram @sonofstars_.

KATHARINE JOHNSEN holds an MFA in creative writing from the University of North Carolina Wilmington, where she was the Bernice Kert Fellow, and a BA from Emory University. She is the recipient of a scholarship from the Sewanee Writers' Conference and a Dorothy Sargent Rosenberg Poetry Prize. Her work is forthcoming or has appeared recently in *The Kenyon Review, Five Points, NELLE, Southern Indiana Review,* and elsewhere.

ANDREW DAVID KING is a poet and artist from the East Bay, California. His poems and nonfiction have appeared in print and online with

ZYZZYVA, Poetry, boundary 2, The Kenyon Review, The Rumpus, and more. From 2016 to 2017 he was a Global Academic Fellow at NYU Shanghai. He's presently a student at the Iowa Writers' Workshop.

HANNAH PERRIN KING grew up on a dirt road in rural California and now lives in Brooklyn, New York. She completed her MFA at The New School and is currently an affiliate editor at *The Alaska Quarterly Review.* Mostly recently she became the winner of AWP's 2018 Kurt Brown Prize for Poetry.

CAROL PARRIS KRAUSS is a mother, educator, and poet from the Tidewater region of Virginia. Her work can be found at *Escape into Life, Fall Lines: A Literary Convergence, Story South, The South Carolina Review, Poetry 24, New Verse News, Tuck Magazine, The Amsterdam Quarterly, Pedestal Magazine,* and other online and print venues.

PETER LABERGE is the author of the chapbooks *Makeshift Cathedral* (YesYes Books, 2017) and *Hook* (Sibling Rivalry Press, 2015). He is the founder and editor-in-chief of *The Adroit Journal,* and his work has previously appeared in *Best New Poets, Crazyhorse, Harvard Review, Iowa Review, Pleiades,* and *Tin House.* He lives in San Francisco.

SCOT LANGLAND lives and writes poetry in Birmingham, Alabama. Having recently received his MA from the University of Alabama at Birmingham, he currently teaches English at his alma mater and works on the editorial staffs of *Birmingham Poetry Review* and *NELLE.* When he finds the time, he travels across his corner of the world visiting with kith and kin.

MICHAEL LEE is a Norwegian-American writer, youth worker, and organizer. He has received grants and scholarships from the Minnesota State Arts Board, the LOFT Literary Center, and the Bread Loaf Writers Conference. Winner of the Scotti Merrill Award for poetry from the Key West

Literary Seminar, his poetry has appeared in *Ninth Letter, Hayden's Ferry Review, Indiana Review, Poetry Northwest,* and *Copper Nickel* among others. Michael lives and works in North Minneapolis where he spends his free time reading and working in his garden.

ELIZABETH LEMIEUX comes from small town in Maine where churches outnumber traffic lights. Her work has appeared in *The Best Teen Writing of 2015, Maine Magazine,* as well as in her poetry chapbook, *The Presumpscot Baptism of a Jewish Girl.*

CHELSEA LISTON is a Utahan currently studying and teaching poetry at Arizona State University in Tempe. Her most recent work has appeared or is forthcoming in *BOAAT* and *Passages North.* She is a poetry editor at *Hayden's Ferry Review* and *Spilled Milk Magazine.*

JENNIE MALBOEUF is a native of Kentucky. Her poems are found in *The Southern Review, Harvard Review, The Gettysburg Review, Virginia Quarterly Review, Prairie Schooner,* and *FIELD.* She teaches at Guilford College in North Carolina.

LORENA PARKER MATEJOWSKY lives in Central Florida with her husband and three children, but spent her first thirty years in Texas. Her poetry was selected for the 2018 AWP Intro Journal Prize and has also appeared in *Tinderbox, Rise Up Review, Sinking City,* and more. She reads for *The Florida Review* and is an MFA in creative writing student at the University of Central Florida.

T. J. MCLEMORE's poems, interviews, and reviews appear in *The Adroit Journal, Crazyhorse, 32 Poems, Michigan Quarterly Review, Kenyon Review Online, Poetry Daily,* and other publications. He is the recipient of the Richard Peterson Poetry Prize from *Crab Orchard Review,* a Pushcart Prize nomination, and a scholarship from the Sewanee Writers' Conference. He is an English doctoral student at the University of Colorado–Boulder.

KRISTEN RENEE MILLER is a poet, editor, and translator based in Louisville, Kentucky. Her work has appeared or is forthcoming in *Poetry*, *The Kenyon Review*, *Guernica*, *The Offing*, and elsewhere. She is the translator of *Spawn*, a poetry collection by Ilnu Nation poet Marie-Andrée Gill, forthcoming in 2019. Kristen is the managing editor at Sarabande Books, where she also directs Sarabande Writing Labs, a program that hosts creative writing workshops in partnership with social-service nonprofits.

ERIKA MUELLER is a mother and AmeriCorps alumna. She received her PhD from the University of Wisconsin–Milwaukee, MFA from the University of Oregon, and MA from Iowa State University. Her poems have appeared in *Colorado Review*, *Crab Orchard Review*, and *Midwest Review*, among others.

OLATUNDE OSINAIKE is a Nigerian-American poet and software developer from the West Side of Chicago. A *Best of the Net* and *Bettering American Poetry* nominee, his most recent work has appeared, or is forthcoming, in *Kweli*, *Glass: A Journal of Poetry*, *Cosmonauts Avenue*, *Lunch Ticket*, *Puerto del Sol*, and *Columbia Poetry Review*, among other publications. He is currently on poetry staff at *The Adroit Journal* and you can find him at olatundeosinaike.com.

WILLY PALOMO is the son of two immigrants from El Salvador. He is a McNair Scholar, Macondista, and a Frost Place Latin@ Scholar. He has performed his poetry (inter)nationally at the National Poetry Slam, CUPSI, and V Festival Internacional de Poesía Amada Libertad in El Salvador. His poems and reviews have been featured in *Latino Rebels*, *Muzzle*, *The Wandering Song: Central American Writing in the United States*, and more. His first collection of poetry is forthcoming from Black Lawrence Press. Follow him @palomopoemas and palomopoemas.com.

TYLER ALLEN PENNY is a bi poet, performer, and educator from a one stoplight town in the pine belt of Mississippi. His poems can be found in *Columbia Journal, TSR: The Southampton Review, Deep South Magazine, Salt Journal, OF ZOOS,* and *Fearsome Critters: A Millennial Arts Journal.* He is the recipient of the Joseph Kelly Prize and scholarships to attend artist residencies at Taleamor Park, The Vermont Studio Center and *Tin House*'s Winter Workshop. In 2017, he received his MFA in creative writing and literature from Stony Brook Southampton, where he taught undergraduate poetry courses, as well as high school playwriting courses for the Young Artists and Writers Project. You can reach him at tylerallenpenny.com.

BARRY PETERS is a writer and teacher in Durham, North Carolina. Recent/forthcoming work appears in *The American Journal of Poetry, Baltimore Review, Broad River Review, The Cabinet of Heed, Connecticut River Review, The Healing Muse, Jelly Bucket, Miramar, Plainsongs, Rattle, South Florida Poetry Journal, The Southampton Review,* and *Sport Literate.*

MEGHANN PLUNKETT is a poet living in New York City. Her work has previously appeared in *Narrative Magazine, Third Coast, Pleiades, Rattle,* and *Washington Square Review,* among others. She was the winner of the 2017 Missouri Review Editors' Prize as well as the winner of the 2017 Third Coast Poetry Prize. She serves as a poetry reader for *The New Yorker.*

FORREST RAPIER is the recipient of a University Poetry Prize. His work is forthcoming in *The Greensboro Review* and *Saw Palm.*

PHOEBE REEVES earned her MFA at Sarah Lawrence College and teaches English at the University of Cincinnati's Clermont College in rural southern Ohio. She has had poems appear in *The Gettysburg Review; Hayden's Ferry Review; Forklift, Ohio; Phoebe;* and *Memorious.*

CARLY RUBIN is a poet currently living in Louisiana. She earned her MFA from the City College of New York–CUNY and is now a PhD candidate in English literature at Louisiana State University, where she writes about lyric poetry and modern physics (which, as it turns out, aren't so different after all). Her creative work has appeared in *Analog Magazine*, on NPR's *RadioLab*, and elsewhere. She also occasionally writes for the *Harvard Review Online*. Find her at carlymarierubin.wordpress.com.

SHAKTHI SHRIMA's work appears or is forthcoming in *VINYL*, *The Adroit Journal*, *Tinderbox*, *BOAAT*, *Muzzle*, *DIALOGIST*, *inter\rupture*, and *Berkeley Poetry Review*, among others. Shakthi Shrima is forthcoming in her unmade bed. Find her at shakthishrima.com.

CRAIG VAN ROOYEN's poems have appeared in *32 Poems*, *Narrative*, *New Ohio Review*, *Southern Humanities Review*, *Southern Poetry Review*, *Rattle*, *Willow Springs*, and elsewhere. He is winner of the 2014 Rattle Poetry Prize and has an MFA in poetry from Pacific University.

JAMES A.H. WHITE is a gay, Japanese-British writer based in Maryland. Winner of an AWP Intro Journals Project award, his writing can be found in *Best New British & Irish Poets 2018* (selected by Maggie Smith), *Black Warrior Review*, *Colorado Review*, *Lambda Literary*, and *Washington Square Review*, among many other publications. The author of *hiku [pull]*, a chapbook (Porkbelly Press), he received his MFA in creative writing from Florida Atlantic University, where he was a Lawrence A. Sanders fellow.

AMY WOOLARD is a writer and legal aid attorney working on justice and poverty policy and legislation in Virginia. Her forthcoming debut poetry collection, *Neck of the Woods*, received the 2018 Alice James Award from Alice James Books. Her poems have appeared in publications such as *The New Yorker*, *Boston Review*, *Ploughshares*, *Fence*, *Virginia Quarterly Review*, and the *Best New Poets 2013* and *2015* anthologies, among others; her essays and reporting have appeared in *Slate*, *The Guardian*, *Pacific Standard*, and *The Rumpus*, as well as *Virginia Quarterly Review*, which awarded her the Staige D. Blackford Prize for Nonfiction in 2016. She lives in Charlottesville, Virginia.

Participating Magazines

32 Poems
32poems.com

The Account
theaccountmagazine.com

The Adroit Journal
theadroitjournal.org

AGNI Magazine
bu.edu/agni

The American Journal of Poetry
theamericanjournalofpoetry.com

The Antioch Review
review.antiochcollege.edu

Apple Valley Review
applevalleyreview.com

apt
apt.aforementionedproductions
.com

ARTS & LETTERS
artsandletters.gcsu.edu

Atlanta Review
atlantareview.com

Atticus Review
atticusreview.org

The Believer
believermag.com

Bennington Review
benningtonreview.org

Birmingham Poetry Review
uab.edu/cas/englishpublications/
birmingham-poetry-review

The Bitter Oleander
bitteroleander.com

Blackbird
blackbird.vcu.edu

Black Warrior Review
bwr.ua.edu

Blood Orange Review
bloodorangereview.com

The Boiler Journal
theboilerjournal.com

The Bookends Review
thebookendsreview.com

Booth: A Journal
booth.butler.edu

Boulevard
boulevardmagazine.org

Boxcar Poetry Review
boxcarpoetry.com

Brick
brickmag.com

cahoodaloodaling
cahoodaloodaling.com

Carve Magazine
carvezine.com

Cincinnati Review
cincinnatireview.com

The Collagist
thecollagist.com

The Collapsar
thecollapsar.org

Connotation Press
connotationpress.com

Copper Nickel
copper-nickel.org

Crab Fat Magazine
crabfatmagazine.com

Crab Orchard Review
craborchardreview.siu.edu

Crazyhorse
crazyhorse.cofc.edu

Cutthroat
cutthroatmag.com

Diode
diodepoetry.com

Ecotone
ecotonemagazine.org

EVENT Magazine
eventmagazine.ca

Every Pigeon
everypigeon.com

Foglifter
foglifterjournal.com

Foothill: A Journal of Poetry
cgu.edu/foothill

Foundry
foundryjournal.com

Free State Review
freestatereview.com

The Georgia Review
thegeorgiareview.com

Gettysburg Review
gettysburgreview.com

Glass: A Journal of Poetry
glass-poetry.com/journal.html

Grist: A Journal of the Literary Arts
gristjournal.com

Guernica
guernicamag.com

Hamilton Arts & Letters
HALmagazine.com

Hot Metal Bridge
hotmetalbridge.org

Image
imagejournal.org

Jabberwock Review
jabberwock.org.msstate.edu

Jelly Bucket
jellybucket.org

The Lascaux Review
lascauxreview.com

Lunch Ticket
lunchticket.org

Memorious: A Journal of New Verse
& Fiction
memorious.org

Mid-American Review
casit.bgsu.edu/midamericanreview

MORIA Literary Magazine
moriaonline.com

Muzzle Magazine
muzzlemagazine.com

The Nashville Review
as.vanderbilt.edu/nashvillereview

New England Review
nereview.com

Nimrod International Journal
utulsa.edu/nimrod

Ninth Letter
ninthletter.com

Pacifica Literary Review
pacificareview.com

Passages North
passagesnorth.com

Pembroke Magazine
pembrokemagazine.com

Penn Review
pennreview.org

Phoebe
phoebejournal.com

Ploughshares
pshares.org

The Pinch
pinchjournal.com

Puerto del Sol
puertodelsol.org

Quarterly West
quarterlywest.com

Raleigh Review
RaleighReview.org

Rascal
rascaljournal.com

Rattle
rattle.com

Redivider
redividerjournal.org

Roanoke Review
roanokereview.org

Ruminate Magazine
ruminatemagazine.com

Salamander
salamandermag.org

Saw Palm: Florida Literature & Art
sawpalm.org

The Shallow Ends
theshallowends.com

The Southeast Review
southeastreview.org

Southern Indiana Review
usi.edu/sir

The Southern Review
thesouthernreview.org

Split Lip
splitlipmagazine.com

Sugar House Review
SugarHouseReview.com

Sundog Lit
sundoglit.com

Tahoma Literary Review
tahomaliteraryreview.com

Thrush Poetry Journal
thrushpoetryjournal.com

Tinderbox Poetry Journal
tinderboxpoetry.com

The Tishman Review
thetishmanreview.com

TRACK//FOUR
trackfourjournal.com

Up North Lit
upnorthlit.org

upstreet
upstreet-mag.org

Up the Staircase Quarterly
upthestaircase.org

Virginia Quarterly Review
vqronline.org

Washington Square Review
washingtonsquarereview.com

Waxwing Literary Journal
waxwingmag.org

Whale Road Review
whaleroadreview.com

wildness
readwildness.com

Willow Springs
willowspringsmagazine.org

Winter Tangerine
wintertangerine.com

Yemassee
yemasseejournal.com

Zone 3
zone3press.com

Participating Programs

Chatham University MFA in Creative Writing
chatham.edu/mfa

Creighton University MFA in Creative Writing
creighton.edu/program/creative-writing-mfa

Florida International University MFA in Creative Writing
english.fiu.edu/creative-writing

Florida State University Creative Writing
english.fsu.edu/programs/creative-writing

George Mason University MFA in Creative Writing
creativewriting.gmu.edu

Hollins University Jackson Center for Creative Writing
hollinsmfa.wordpress.com

Johns Hopkins The Writing Seminars
writingseminars.jhu.edu

Kansas State University MFA in Creative Writing Program
k-state.edu/english/programs/cw

McNeese State University MFA Program
mfa.mcneese.edu

Minnesota State University Mankato Creative Writing Program
english.mnsu.edu/cw/index.html

Monmouth University Creative Writing
monmouth.edu/school-of-humanities-social-sciences/ma-english.aspx

Mount Saint Mary's University MFA in Creative Writing
msmu.edu/creativewriting

New Mexico Highlands University MA in English (Creative Writing)
nmhu.edu/current-students/graduate/arts-and-sciences/english

New School Writing Program
newschool.edu/writing

New York University Creative Writing Program
as.nyu.edu/cwp

North Carolina State MFA in Creative Writing
english.chass.ncsu.edu/graduate/mfa

Northwestern University MA/MFA in Creative Writing
sps.northwestern.edu/program-areas/graduate/creative-writing

The Ohio State University MFA Program in Creative Writing
english.osu.edu/mfa

Ohio University Creative Writing PhD
ohio.edu/cas/english/grad/creative-writing/index.cfm

Pacific University Master of Fine Arts in Writing
pacificu.edu/as/mfa

San Diego State University MFA in Creative Writing
mfa.sdsu.edu

Sarah Lawrence College MFA in Writing
sarahlawrence.edu/writing-mfa

Syracuse University MFA in Creative Writing
english.syr.edu/cw/cw-program.html

Texas Tech University Creative Writing Program
depts.ttu.edu/english/cw

UMass Amherst MFA for Poets and Writers
umass.edu/englishmfa

UMass Boston MFA Program in Creative Writing
umb.edu/academics/cla/english/grad/mfa

University of Alabama at Birmingham Graduate Theme in Creative Writing
uab.edu/cas/english/graduate-program/creative-writing

University of British Columbia Creative Writing Program
creativewriting.ubc.ca

University of Connecticut Creative Writing Program
creativewriting.uconn.edu

University of Idaho MFA in Creative Writing
uidaho.edu/class/english/graduate/mfa-creative-writing

University of Illinois at Chicago Program for Writers
engl.uic.edu/CW

University of Kansas Graduate Creative Writing Program
http://englishcw.ku.edu/

University of Maryland MFA Program
english.umd.edu

University of Michigan Helen Zell Writers' Program
lsa.umich.edu/writers

University of Mississippi MFA in Creative Writing
mfaenglish.olemiss.edu

University of Missouri Creative Writing Program
english.missouri.edu/area/creative-writing

University of New Orleans Creative Writing Workshop
uno.edu/writing

University of North Texas Creative Writing
english.unt.edu/creative-writing-0

University of Notre Dame Creative Writing Program
english.nd.edu/creative-writing

University of South Florida MFA in Creative Writing
english.usf.edu/graduate/concentrations/cw/degrees

University of Texas Michener Center for Writers
michener.utexas.edu

Vermont College of Fine Arts MFA in Writing
vcfa.edu

Virginia Tech MFA in Creative Writing Program
liberalarts.vt.edu/academics/graduate-programs/masters-programs-list/
    master-of-fine-arts-in-creative-writing.html

Western Michigan University Master of Fine Arts in Creative Writing
wmich.edu/english

West Virginia University MFA Program
creativewriting.wvu.edu

*The series editor wishes to thank the many poets involved in our
first round of reading:*

*Sara Brickman, Helena Chung, Michaela Cowgill, Michael Dhyne,
Landis Grenville, Valencia Grice, Emily Lawson, Emily Nason,
Caleb Nolen, Sean Shearer, Anna Tomlinson, and Sasha Prevost.*

*Special thanks to Jason Coleman and the University of Virginia Press
for editorial advice and support.*